Magic of Irises

BARBARA PERRY LAWTON

FULCRUM PUBLISHING

For Becca and Graham,
with thanks for their boundless enthusiasm!

Library of Congress Cataloging-in-Publication Data

Lawton, Barbara Perry.
    Magic of Irises / Barbara Perry Lawton.
            p.   cm.
    Includes bibliographical references and index.
    ISBN 1-55591-267-2 (hc)
    1. Iris (Plant) I. Title
SB413.I8L39   1998
635.9'3438—dc21   97-40543
                                                   CIP

Printed and bound in Korea
by Sung In Printing Company

0 9 8 7 6 5 4 3 2 1

Fulcrum Publishing
350 Indiana Street, Suite 350
Golden, Colorado 80401-5093 USA
(800) 992-2908 • (303) 277-1623
website: www.fulcrum-gardening.com
e-mail: fulcrum@fulcrum-gardening.com

Table of Contents

Iris stylosa.

Iris siberica.

Acknowledgments

I want to thank many of the American Iris Society members who have taken a great deal of time and effort to help me with research and generously shared their knowledge and experience. Ann Lowe was generous with information on historic irises. Anna Mae Miller was helpful with the chapter on Siberian irises. Lewis and Adele Lawyer were kind enough to verify my Pacific Coast iris information and also furnish other information I needed. Clarence Mahan checked the information on Japanese irises. Jean and Jim Morris have helped in many ways, from checking the accuracy of information to sharing their garden. Dave Niswonger was very encouraging and checked my work on spuria irises. Bob Pries also helped by suggesting resources and checking the accuracy of iris information including particularly the species irises. Riley Probst has encouraged and helped me with advice and information on many occasions. Melody Wilhoit helped with the chapter on Louisiana irises. Pat Williamson has pointed me in the right directions and provided sound advice. Connie Wolf of the Missouri Botanical Garden Library paved the way for me to use the library's extensive collections. The St. Louis Art Museum was valuable for researching how irises have fit into the world of art.

Introduction

Bearded irises are the first garden flowers I remember as a small child. I must have been about four when I first saw the elegant purple, gold and tawny brown irises growing along the edge of our city yard next to a cinder-block garage and along the edge of the two-family stucco house where we lived.

Although the garage itself was drab and ugly and the house hardly an award winner, the irises in both bright and subtle shades were breathtaking, even in that location. They were not cared for nor did anyone else seem to admire them but, nonetheless, they continued to bloom and even thrive in that seemingly inhospitable spot. That early experience was enough to make me notice irises forever after.

Since that time, I have grown irises and learned how well they fit into many environments and just about any garden. I quickly learned that they are easy to grow and extremely rewarding. One hot, droughty summer in St. Louis I learned through experience that bearded irises are survivors of extreme conditions—I threw some rejected bearded iris rhizomes on a compost pile of leaves and garden waste.

The next spring, there on top of the compost pile were the rejected irises, thriving and blooming their heads off. I'd be willing to bet a nickel cash that irises will provide more beauty for less effort than just about any garden perennials I know.

Other irises came into my garden world as time went on. A planting of Dutch iris bulbs brought spring treats of slim delicate flowers in purple, yellow and white. They were handsome accents along the edge of a stone terrace. Then I discovered the glory of the crested irises and enjoyed them at the edge of a shady garden where they made a mass of heavenly blue each spring. The Siberian irises were my next discovery and I thought I'd found my favorite iris when a cultivar called 'Caesar's Brother' first bloomed in my garden.

'Carriwitched', an intermediate bearded iris, is shown here in an Oregon garden. (Photograph by Jim Morris.)

Today, I realize that I have only touched the edge of the iris world. There are more species and horticultural types of iris than I will ever grow. Fortunately, there are botanical gardens, display gardens and lots of iris fanciers who grow them. I continue to be one of the great admirers of irises in gardens wherever I go.

When I first thought about writing a book about irises, it was because I wanted to know more about this elegant group of plants. What better way to learn about something than to write about it. I talked to a few of the experts and was astounded by their enthusiasm for my project. I'm more used to a "That's nice" response, but the iris people said things like "What a great idea!" and "We need good up-to-date American books on irises." Needless to say, that has spurred my enthusiasm.

Since then, I have gone to many of the specialists within the American Iris Society, as well as to growers and others who are more than ordinarily aware of the irises. Without exception, they have been very helpful in filling in many specific details about irises for me to pass on to you. I am particularly grateful to many members of the American Iris Society and the Kirkwood Iris Society for their help and encouragement.

Along the way, I have joined the American Iris Society and also joined all of its various sections. Each section has its own president and membership secretary and its own periodical publication. These are a great aid in helping one gain knowledge about the many members of the genus *Iris*. A local friend, who has been involved with irises for several years more than I have, has been immensely generous in pointing me in several right directions.

As luck would have it, we have a surprisingly large group of iris experts in our Missouri-Illinois region, including knowledgeable iris show judges, iris breeders, and both amateur and lettered botanists experienced in the classification, origin and culture of irises. As I did the research needed for this book, I found myself increasingly fascinated with the irises to such a degree that I am now going to all the iris meetings I can find the time for, and am even signing up for judging courses—what better way to learn the particulars of both horticultural and species irises than to see them demonstrated by the experts.

The organization of this book, as far as the various kinds of irises are concerned, is based upon the American Iris Society's sections. These sections and cooperating societies are more specific. There are special groups for median, Siberian, spuria, Japanese, reblooming, dwarf, Pacific Coast native, species, historic, aril and Louisiana irises. Some of these sections, such as the Median Iris Society, which focuses on bearded irises of a certain size, are based upon horticultural specifics of the plants. Others, including the societies for Japanese and Siberian irises, are based upon botanical classifications.

Because this book is dedicated to helping gardeners learn more about irises, my descriptions are based on the *Handbook for Judges and Show Officials* of the American Iris Society. The ideal sizes, forms, colors—indeed, everything about the plants—are defined in this book. Each iris in a show, or in the garden, is judged for its flower, flower stalk, distinctiveness and the plant as a whole. I include these criteria for each kind of iris since they are excellent ways for any gardener to evaluate plants for his or her own garden.

A high-quality iris plant has crisp erect leaves that are appropriately wide for its type and are of good color. It should be a vigorous, durable plant that flowers well for three or more growing seasons without being divided. It should provide abundant blooms and remain in bloom for over two weeks. The flower stalk should be in scale with the rest of the plant and sufficiently strong to support the flowers. It should carry the flowers above the foliage, but not too high above it. The flower stalk should branch openly in a way that doesn't allow the blooms to interfere with one another or with the branches of other plants. The iris flower will earn points for good clear color, substance and durability.

The desirable flower form, including the shape, structure and position of the petals, should be balanced and in proportion, while providing an obvious garden beauty. The judging book describes the desired positions of the standards and the falls in great detail. It is worth noting that the desired flower forms of many types of garden irises have changed in recent years.

Enthusiastic gardeners probably won't be particularly interested in my discussions of the botany and classification of irises. Discussions of genetics and chromosome counts may hold little interest except for the truly dedicated. Those whose interests cover all aspects of irises, including the breeding of these beautiful plants, can find some of the necessary botanical details in chapters 26 and 27.

The chapter on breeding irises may capture your interest when you have grown irises for a while. It is interesting to note that the majority of beautiful new iris varieties have been bred by amateur growers. You, too, have an opportunity to breed new irises that may be the stars of tomorrow's gardens.

As I've learned more about irises, I have come to admire them to an even greater degree than before. The flowers are exquisitely beautiful. I cannot think of more handsome blooms than those produced by the many wild and cultivated irises. Likewise, I cannot think of foliage that is more graceful than the swordlike leaves of the irises. There are irises for any garden situation I can think of, from water gardens to perennial borders to rock gardens. It's no wonder that irises have played major roles in history and art.

The research for this book has led me into magical places that I never knew existed. When I was working on iris references and artwork at the St. Louis Art Museum, I wished that I were fluent in Japanese. There were folios of Japanese art, including irises, that were so breathtaking, even in reproduction, that I could barely stand to send them back to the shelves. To my eye, the most awesome were reproductions of paneled screens, with gold leaf surrounding the flower depictions. Simply gorgeous! If I were immensely rich, I would become a patron of such art.

Whether you call them irises, fleurs-de-lis or flags, irises are worthy plants that deserve at least one planting in every garden. Their linear quality and beautiful flowers make them ideal for use as focal points, contrast, texture and color in ornamental beds or borders of all kinds.

The Lore and Legends of Irises

Irises in History

The fleur-de-lis, although its name translates to "flower of the lily," probably is the name given long ago to the white Florentine iris (*Iris florentina*). Perhaps the iris was once commonly called a lily. Some claim that fleur-de-lis means "flower of Louis," but whatever the origin, there's no question that the fleur-de-lis does represent an iris. It was the respected emblem of French monarchs for many centuries, appearing on flags, tapestries, shields and armor.

Possibly, the use of the iris as a symbol traces back to ancient India and Egypt, where it stood as a symbol of life. Hathor, the ancient Egyptian goddess of heaven, joy, music and love, was the mother of Horus, the god of light and heaven. Horus often was identified with the lotus, symbol of the essence of life, and sometimes was said to have been born of the lotus.

This symbolism eventually extended to the iris and also the lily. These flowers became associated with thunder, one of the destructive powers of Horus. Since the thunder weapon was used to protect the Egyptians, the flowers came to represent the protection of life. So the iris was a symbol of both the essence and the renewal of life. The ancient Egyptians believed that the three petals stood for faith, wisdom and valor. Since the iris flower reflected a sense of authority, it was used to decorate the funeral temples of the pharaohs, who believed the iris would preserve their power in the next life.

There are iris species names—*Iris mesopotamia* and *I. kashmiriana*—that correspond to territories where Alexander the Great's army marched

Iris florentina, a white form of the German iris.

Iris icon on wrought-iron fence.
(Photograph by Jim Morris.)

eastward as far as India in the fourth century B.C. This son of Philip of Macedonia was the first conqueror of Western civilization and as a result was a spearhead of ancient Greek culture. Other irises collected at around the same period reflect places that the Greeks colonized on Turkish shores—*Iris trojana, I. cypriana* and *I. junonia.*

The goddess Iris of Greek mythology was a beloved messenger of the gods, especially of Hera, who became Juno to the ancient Romans. She had golden wings and was the goddess of the rainbow. Iris traveled on the rainbow's arc, carrying commands and messages from the ancient gods to mankind. Iris married the west wind, Zephyrus. To this day, the Greeks plant irises on women's graves, believing that the goddess Iris will guide the souls of women to their last resting places.

In the Christian world, the fleur-de-lis came to be particularly sacred to the Virgin Mary. A legend tells of a knight who could never remember more than the two words *Ave Maria* of the Latin prayer that was said to honor the Holy Mother. Night and day, he continued his supplications with these two words. After many years, the old man died and was buried in the chapel yard of a convent. Proof of the acceptance of his brief but sincere prayer by the Virgin Mary came when a plant of fleur-de-lis grew upon his grave. On each flower, golden letters spelled out *Ave Maria.*

The number three is implicit in the structure of the iris flower and obvious in its three standards and three falls, the six petals of its form. Three has also long been a strong and mystical number, especially in representing the Trinity in Christianity. There were also the three Magi. There are many triple design elements in ecclesiastical art.

The number three represented completion to Pythagoras, the sixth-century B.C. Greek philosopher and mathematician. He thought so because the number three consists of a beginning, middle and end. Three is prominent in Greek mythology, which also offers the three Fates, the three Graces and Cerberus, the three-headed dog. Cerberus lived in the Infernal Regions near the black river Cocytus where Charon served as boatman.

Is there a connection between this mystique of three and the iris? There appears to be a good case for it. The Tri-State Iris Society in Joplin, Missouri, printed a short piece describing iris in terms of three:

Its three petals ever reaching upwards toward heaven represent the Trinity, Father, Son and the Holy Ghost. They also speak of the trinity of man—body, soul and spirit, reaching upward in supplication for guidance. Three petals turn earthward, representing our daily lives, each having a sprinkling of gold, symbolic of deity or God's presence with us every day. With the three upward petals there is another set of three pushing upward in the style crests. These four sets of three symbolize the twelve disciples chosen by Christ.

The first mention of the iris in the history of France occurs during the reign of Clovis I, a Frankish king who became the powerful ruler of the Merovingian dynasty that founded the French state, in A.D. 481. It was Clovis who defeated Rome's last great army in Gaul in 486. He went on to also defeat the Alamanni, the Visigoths and the Burgundians. Within a decade Clovis and the Franks would rule western Germany and the Low Countries of northwestern Europe, as well as most of Gaul.

Legend says that Clovis adopted the fleur-de-lis as his symbol in the early 500s when an angel gave him an iris in honor of his becoming a Christian. Clovis was the first Germanic ruler to become a Christian. Up until that point, most of the Germanic kings were either pagans or Aryan heretics. Clovis earned the valuable support of the Catholic clergy and laymen with his conversion to Christianity.

A few hundred years later, in 1147, the fleur-de-lis was first used as an emblem of French monarchy by an *ordonnance* of Louis le Jeune. Then in 1376, Charles V, known throughout his kingdom of France as Charles the Wise, adopted three fleurs-de-lis for his coat of arms. In addition to being a man of letters who supported both art and literature, Charles V reformed the government that had been torn apart by rivaling factions, built up the army and navy and resumed the Hundred Years' War with England. Since he was successful in all of these ventures, the iris became recognized throughout Europe as a symbolize of the reign of Charles the Wise.

That is how the iris came to be a symbol in the system of heraldry. At first these symbols—the iris, beasts, fish and birds—were simply helpful ways to tell foe from friend in those medieval days when knights were encased in armor. Like Clovis, the knights chose symbols that represented an event or some quality of character. These heraldic symbols were also used as seals to authenticate documents in times when few could read and write.

This very modern iris, the reblooming, tall bearded 'Lichen', ,echoes the traditional form of the fleur-de-lis. (Photograph by Barbara Perry Lawton.)

Once gunpowder was introduced from China, armor was no longer effective, and the symbols of heraldry then were used in elegant emblems created to represent particular families rather than individual knights. The symbols combined to make coats of arms that were created in formal patterns following certain rules of usage. In 1484, the Herald's College or College of Arms was established in England by Richard III. This institution made the decisions as to who qualified to use and wear coats of arms and also what particulars could be used to make a coat of arms. In the code of usage of the Herald's College, the fleur-de-lis is the mark that symbolizes a sixth son on the shields of coats of arms.

Today, in Great Britain and other nations, coats of arms indicate someone's ancestry rather than an event or characteristic. Countries, provinces and states use coats of arms on flags, seals, stationery and other official items. Tennessee adopted the iris as its official state flower in 1933. Three representations of the fleur-de-lis are on Quebec's provincial coat of arms, a tribute to its French heritage.

The fleur-de-lis became common as an artistic symbol. It has shown up as an attractive terminal for the limbs of the cross. Since the fleur-de-lis is an ancient symbol of life, this is appropriate symbolism.

IRISES IN THE WORLD OF ART

Irises first appeared in the artworks of the ancient civilizations of Egypt, Asia Minor and northwestern India before 3000 B.C. The earliest known iris painting was on a wall of the spectacular mountainside Palace of Knossos, which belonged to King Minos of Crete, the largest island in the Aegean Sea. The Minoans, who made up the first civilization in the ancient Greek region, became noted first for learning to make bronze in about 3000 B.C. and then for their shipbuilding and flourishing trade with Egypt. When the Minoans built an elegant palace at Knossos for King Minos, they decorated it with the best of their art, including the stylized fresco of what appear to be life-size bulbous irises, shown on the ground next to Minos, the priest-king of Minoa.

Although the Islamic Arabs of the seventh century A.D. had little art in their own culture, their conquests brought them into close contact with the highly developed cultures of Persia, Syria, Egypt and Mesopotamia. This blend of cultures gave rise to what is known as Islamic art, also known as Mohammedan or Moslem art. In Spain the style is known as Moorish art after the Moslem group that invaded Iberia in the eighth century.

The key to this art, which flourished until the seventeenth century, is that Islam, a strict religion, prohibits the depiction of human beings and animals. They believe that Allah is the one and only creator of life and that any attempt to paint creatures would trespass upon the divine rights of Allah. When they did use people, animals and birds in artwork, they were highly abstracted. Therefore the designs of the artwork in their extraordinarily beautiful temples, textiles, carvings and illustrations depended heavily upon highly stylized floral motifs. The three-part flowers of irises often appear in Islamic art.

Iris latiflora major, *the English iris (a* Xiphium *iris), native to Spain and the Pyrenees.*

7

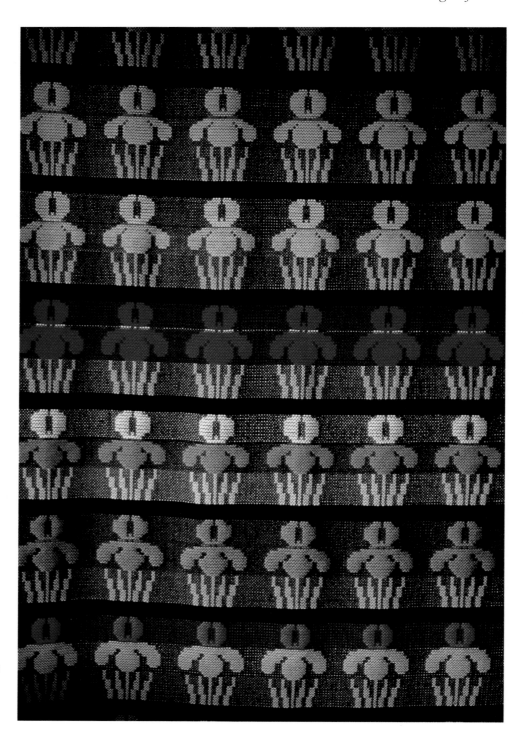

Iris patterns have dominated artwork for more than 5,000 years. In this quilt, the repetitive patterning of the iris is not only beautiful but practical. (Photograph by Jim Morris.)

When Siddhartha Gautama began teaching his great truths, his followers called him Buddha, which means "enlightened" or "wise." After his death, his teachings spread until Buddhism was the major faith in India. By A.D. 100, Buddhism was extending into China and, within a few centuries, it was a major religious force in Korea, Japan and Tibet. Since one of the Buddha's teachings was that man should love nature and that wise men should regard themselves as part of nature, the natural world was a major focus of artwork—paintings, scrolls, poems and screens.

Ogata Korin (1658–1716), who was born in the beautiful city of Kyoto, Japan, represents a great achievement of Japanese art in depicting the natural world. His folding screens, with panels of ink and color on gold-ground paper, were meant to beautify rooms and they certainly must have. Wealthy people of his time and ours could ask for no more beautiful adornment to a room than a Korin screen. His pair of six-fold screens called *Irises at Yatsuhashi* elegantly shows how Korin could turn his subjects into eye-catching designs. His sense of pattern and color is breathtaking.

Another Japanese artist was Watanabe Shiko (1683–1755), sometimes dismissed as a minor follower of Ogata Korin. When the Cleveland Museum of Art acquired a pair of six-fold screens called *Irises,* critics and historians began to have second thoughts. These panoramic views of waves of irises, in ink and color on gold-ground paper, have given Shiko an important spot in the development of eighteenth-century painting. It was he who gave new emphasis to the use of visual reality in painting, a major trend of his time.

Critics point out that Korin, while representing each flower cluster with clarity and freshness, subordinates naturalism to pictorial design. Korin, in other words, has imposed his own sense of vision and order upon nature. Shiko, on the other hand, emphasizes exact shapes and intricate details. The critics suggest that while Korin's irises give an impression of vigorous growth, Shiko's irises show delicacy and a transitory feeling. As for me, I find the works of both artists astoundingly beautiful even in reproduction.

Sienese and Florentine painters of the late thirteenth century marked the birth of Western painting in the modern world. It was they who changed from mosaic as the major medium to fresco and tempera painting. Giotto, da Vinci and Michelangelo led the art trend, presenting realistic images of Christ, the Virgin, saints and other religious figures in idealized settings.

Symbols such as the dove, representing the Holy Ghost, and the halos symbolizing holiness occur throughout their monumental works. Common in these paintings are flowers and foliage, often including the iris. Next time you visit an art museum, look for irises in the old religious paintings. Irises also often appeared in fifteenth-century French tapestries.

The seventeenth-century vogue for flower painting conquered all of western Europe, particularly the Low Countries and Dutch Provinces. The establishment of the large horticultural center in Frankfurt-on-the-Main encouraged plant connoisseurs who traveled from all over to find rare plants. Paintings were mostly of bouquets in containers, and irises of blue or lavender were a common component.

Albrecht Dürer (1471–1528) brought plant study to its realistic maturity in his paintings and engravings. He was a part of the new wave of art that represented a return to naturalism. His painting *Iris* was probably of *Iris trojana*. The accuracy of the form with its white standards, lavender falls and yellow beards makes identification possible. Dürer both understood and conveyed a great deal about the structure, form and texture in his magnificent works of art.

Vincent van Gogh (1853–1890) put irises in the world of modern art when he painted *Irises* in 1899, shortly after he voluntarily committed himself to the asylum of Saint-Paul-de-Mausole near the small town of Saint-Remy-de-Provence, a few kilometers from Arles. Only a week after arriving, he wrote to his brother Theo, reporting that he was painting some violet irises that bloomed by the roadside. That canvas turned out to be *Irises* (see page 12). This masterpiece was but one of some 130 that van Gogh completed during the year at Saint Paul.

When *Irises* was first exhibited, the symbolist critic Felix Feneon observed in his review that "the *Irises* violently slash their petals to pieces upon sword-like leaves." Contemporary artist Joan S. Lasher noted in an April 1992 issue of *American Artist:*

> The painting gives the impression that Van Gogh stumbled—literally—onto this composition. Our eyes hurtle into the thick tangle of flowers and leaves, and are at first bewildered by the interlocking blossoms. Form and color are so tightly interwoven that the background seems to have the same depth as the foreground. The overall effect is to flatten the picture plane into a more Oriental perspective—not surprising, considering how Van Gogh was influenced by Japanese woodblock prints.

Vincent van Gogh's Irises, *one of several paintings of irises, 1899. (Courtesy of Netherland Flower Bulb Information Center.)*

In April 1990, *Irises* finally found a permanent home in the Getty Museum in Malibu, California. The painting had been known as the "Curse of the Outback" after it was bought in November 1987 for $53.9 million by Alan Bond, an Australian conglomerator and promoter. Thus the most expensive painting ever sold came to reside in Perth for a time. When Bond's shaky empire collapsed two years later, Sotheby's, the world-famous art auction house, repossessed *Irises* and tried to find a private buyer at a price of $65 million. When these efforts failed, Sotheby's sold the painting to the Getty Museum at an undisclosed price. Art gurus suggest that it is unlikely that the Getty paid more than $40 million, but the actual price remains one of the art world's best-kept secrets.

Prior to the record-breaking sale of *Irises*, the painting had been owned by John Whitney Payson, who inherited it from his parents. His mother had bought *Irises* when he was only seven some forty years before. Payson saw the painting at Sotheby's New York office in 1988 after it had been away on exhibition for the previous three years. He said that seeing it again was such an emotional experience that he felt tears come to his eyes, according to Calvin Tomkins in his article in the April 1988 *New Yorker.*

Payson said the painting had become too expensive to keep, even though he originally had planned to have it on permanent loan to the gallery at Westbrook College. He planned for it to eventually become a gift to the college. According to the same article, Payson said that "the recent and unprecedented spiral in art prices," together with changes in the tax law on donated artworks, had forced him to reevaluate his plans.

Irises is so admired that even fakes bring a lot of money. Artists skilled in the techniques of the original masters hand paint copies that only experts can distinguish from the original. *Irises* is one of the most sought-after re-creations being hand painted by skillful artisans. A recent copy—the companies that market these reproductions prefer that we call them "re-creations"—sold for $10,000.

Georgia O'Keeffe's (1887–1986) flowers are close-up ideations of flowers rather than realistic paintings with every detail and shadow in place. She brought her flower subjects closer and closer to the canvas until the paintings could not hold all of a single bloom. Her search for the perfect flower painting reached its peak in 1926 with the completion of the 30-x-36-inch *Black Iris*. The luminescent *Black Iris* was one of her own favorite works.

Van Gogh's Irises, *the most famous of his iris paintings, is a hallmark of the beauty of the flower captured in art. (Courtesy of the Getty Museum.)*

O'Keeffe became the first American woman artist to succeed alongside men and became for many women a guiding light, according to her husband, the photographer and art impresario Alfred Stieglitz. Critic Henry McBride said that O'Keeffe's color "outblazed" that of other painters in the successful Stieglitz stable of artists.

Her many fans imagined both male and female genitalia in her large flower paintings. According to biographer Jeffrey Hogrefe, O'Keeffe "denied to her last breath that she had meant to depict women's genitalia when she painted a detailed cross-section of an iris that looked vaginal to most eyes." Critic Linda Nochlin argued in the February 1974 *Arts Magazine* that "it is not so much that one stands for the other, but rather that the two meanings are almost interchangeable." For most of her life, O'Keeffe escaped the New York world, seeking solitude in New Mexico where she painted her masterpieces and occupied a "world with no one in it."

Black Iris combines the sensual and the spiritual experience. The arching of the upper petals pulls the viewer's eye into the heart of the flower with its cathedral-like form. O'Keeffe herself said of her flower paintings that they were "like huge buildings going up. People will be startled—they'll have to look at them—and they did." The translucence of the light upper petals and dark lower petals of *Black Iris* are subtle tones. The whole flower is dynamic and appears to be lighted from within. O'Keeffe painted many other flowers and even other irises, but *Black Iris* remains among her greatest works.

George Gessert is a contemporary artist who conceived of and created *The Iris Project* at the University of Oregon Museum of Art in Eugene. In 1981, Gessert happened upon a vigorous colony of Pacific Coast irises beside the Peninsula Road access to Fall Creek Reservoir in west-central Oregon. Captivated by the diversity of the wild irises, he took several specimens back to the university for positive identification. This was the beginning of his quest into "painting with DNA." He uses *Iris tenax, I. innominata* and *I. douglasiana* in his breeding experiments.

Some sixty pots of irises are arranged around a reflecting pool at the museum. In this heterogeneous site with its fountain and life-size bronze of an Indian maiden, the understated irises are an elegant success, according to critic David Stairs. Every day, Gessert attends the irises, watering, culling and cross-pollinating his creation in progress.

Gessert is in the front rank of contemporary artists working in live media. His irises are an integral part of his ongoing research into what he calls the cultural ramifications of human intervention into the evolutionary chain. A graphic artist, Gessert studied horticulture at Oregon State University before joining the Graphic Arts Services Department at the University of Oregon in Eugene.

IRISES AS MEDICINALS AND HOUSEHOLD HERBS

The Greek physician Dioscorides of Anazarbos in Cilicia wrote his herbal *De Materia Medica* in the first century A.D. For the next fifteen centuries he would be the chief resource and inspiration for herbalists and physicians throughout the Western world. He included two irises, *Iris Germanica* and *I. florentina*, in the group he called "The Aromatics." He said,

> Iris is soe named from the resemblance of the rainbow in heaven, but it beares leaves like unto a little sword but greater & braoder & fatter: the flowers on the stalke, are bended in, one ouer against another, & diuers, for they are wither soon white or pale or black or purple or azure. Whence for the varietie of colours it is likened to the heauenly rainebow. The rootes uner are knotty, strong, of a sweet savour, which after the cutting ought to be dryed in the shade, & soe (with a linnen thread put through them) to be layd vp.

He goes on to list the medicinal virtues of the iris:

> All of them haue a warming, extenuating facultie, fitting against coughs, & extenuating grosse humors hard to get up. They purge thick humors & choler, being dranck in Hydromel to the quantity of seven dragms they are also causers of sleep & prouokers of tears & heale the torments of ye belly. But dranck with vinegar they help such as are bitten by venomous beasts, and the splenitick and such as are troubled with convulsion fitts, & such as are chilled, & stiff with cold, & such as let fall their food. But dranck with wine, they bring out the menses, yea, & the decodtion of them is fitting for women's fomentations which doe mollify & open the places, & for

An Iris germanica, one of the many cultivated varieties.

Iris germanica varieties are the best known of the bearded irises, shown here in an Illinois garden. (Photograph by Jim Morris.)

the Sciatica being taken by way of infusion, & for Fistulas, & all hollow sores, which it fill up with flesh.

Dioscorides describes *Iris pseudacorus*, also called "acorum" or "akoron," as having narrower leaves than the previous iris and with similar roots. "The roote hath an heating power, & the decoction thereof dranck, moueth vrina. It is good for the paine of ye Latus, & of the Thorax, & of the Hepare, for ye Tormen, for the Ruptures, for the Convulsions, it abates the Spleen, & it helpes the sick of ye Stillicidium, & them that are a beluis venenatis demorsi."

More than a thousand years later, irises are again described in a famous herbal written by an eminent barber-surgeon of London named John Gerard (1545–1612).

> The root of the common Floure de-luce cleane washed and damped with a few drops of Rose water, and laid plaister-wise upon the face of man or woman, doth in two days at the most take away the blackness or blewness of any stroke or bruse: so that if the skinne of the same woman or any other person be very tender and deli-cate, it shall be needfull that ye lay a piece of silke, sindall, or a piece of fine laune between the plaister and the skinne; for other-wise in such tender bodies it often causeth heate and inflammation.

So says *The Herbal or General History of Plants* by Gerard, which first appeared in 1597. This monumental tome of Renaissance botany contains a consider-able amount of information and handsome illustrations of several irises.

The *Herbal* also recommends iris roots for shortness of breath, an old cough and other chest ailments. Iris root was said to remedy convulsions, cramps and serpent bites. Roots of the German iris were given as a purge. Other irises were said to cure dropsy (edema) and to strengthen sinews and joints. Roots of the bulbous irises, when mixed with goat suet and something called "oile of Alcanna," was supposed to take away the pain of gout.

To this day, orris root from *Iris florentina, I. germanica* and *I. pallida* is used as a scent fixative in potpourri. Of these three, the Florentine iris has the strongest fragrance. Since early times, herbalists have recommended harvest-ing the rhizomes for drying in the early fall. The violetlike scent will grow in strength and last many years. The enduring violet scent is the favorite of per-fume manufacturers looking for the sweet violet fragrance.

Orris root has long been used as a household herb. Since biblical times,

Iris pseudacorus, the yellow flag iris, is best grown in shallow-water sites. This cultivar is 'Flore Pleno', shown here in a Pennsylvania garden. (Photograph by Jim Morris.)

16

the powdered root has been added to laundry rinse water and used to make linens and clothing sweet smelling. In medieval times, especially in Great Britain and northern Europe, the leaves of the iris known as sweet flag were used as a strewing herb to keep the home from smelling musty and dirty. Another household use for an iris is as a dye. The yellow flowers of the plant known as yellow flag (*I. pseudacorus*) will make a yellow dye when steeped. The rhizomes will make a gray or black dye when mordanted with iron.

Many modern herbalists use powdered orris root in combination with such things as rose petals, clove carnation petals, cinnamon and cloves as part of sachet mixes for linen closets, closet shelves and bureau drawers.

All of the irises that have been tested are strong emetics. In the past, this purgative property led to iris rhizomes being used medicinally but modern medicine warns against that practice. The blue flags (*Iris versicolor*) of eastern North America's marshes and wet meadows are dangerously toxic. In spite of that, the dried, powdered rhizomes once had many uses in folk medicine, including the treatment of blood and liver diseases, skin diseases, rheumatism and syphilis. Native Americans used the blue flag as a poultice for treating sores and bruises.

The yellow flag (*Iris pseudacorus*) of Europe also is poisonous and will cause severe abdominal pain and nausea if taken in large amounts. In early times this iris was used as an emetic, diuretic and purgative. Early folk medicine practitioners used the yellow flag for making a cooling astringent liquid for application to wounds. A tea made from the root was used to treat certain gynecological conditions.

In more recent times, a wild iris of western North America (*Iris missouriensis*) has been used to treat toothache. The person with the toothache would hold pulped raw rhizome against the painful area. Since most irises have an emetic and purgative nature, other treatments would be much safer. The emetic nature of irises led to their being a folk medicine used to expel tapeworms. The volatile fragrant oils of some irises are among the many ingredients used for scenting cosmetics, salves, soaps and shampoos. Some people have used roasted iris seeds as coffee substitutes—again, I'm sure there are safer and better coffee substitutes.

Iris missouriensis, *shown here in a Nebraska garden, is native to western North America and is a species known to American gardens. (Photograph by Jim Morris.)*

HISTORY OF IRISES
IN THE GARDEN

It's far easier to trace the story of irises in art than in the garden. Gardeners are not always good record keepers and gardens without attention soon return to some semblance of their original state. As people conquered and explored the world, they would often admire the plants of the invaded land, then take them home or on to other new lands. Some of the more beautiful and unusual of plants, including the irises, traveled to many lands.

The first record of irises in the garden appears to be around 1479 B.C., sometime after King Thutmose III of Egypt conquered Syria. He had a plant specialist on his staff whose duty it was to find new plants for the king. King Thutmose III, who was a gardener, is said to have coveted plants the way some men covet gold. He wanted the flowers he saw in Syria—irises, tulips, lilies, roses and crocuses—to be taken home and planted in his own garden. Once the flowers were blooming in Egypt, he decided to commemorate his conquest of Syria by including flowers in his Temple of Amon at Karnak. To this day, sculptures of irises and the other captured flowers are on the temple wall.

During the twelfth-century Crusades, Louis VII of France arrived in Egypt, where he saw irises growing. It was he who adopted the iris as a symbol of his conquest and carried it back to France. He had the first fleur-de-lis carved on his coat of arms.

Irises are native to the Northern Hemisphere and will only reach their greatest perfection in the North Temperate Zone (but will grow in the Southern Hemisphere). Irises grow to their southern limit on North Africa's coast and no farther south than that. One of the ice ages probably pushed them to

The arilbred iris 'Martha Mia' shown here at the Missouri Botanical Gardens. (Photograph by Barbara Perry Lawton.)

that limit. The northern limit of irises is in northeastern Asia, the Gaspé Peninsula and Alaska.

Ancient Rome had its beginnings in the sixth century B.C. and, over the next several centuries, grew to encompass most of what is now Europe, North Africa and the countries on the eastern end of the Mediterranean Sea. By the end of the second century A.D., the Roman Empire had conquered the Mediterranean lands and encircled the sea, including Egypt and Syria where many irises grew. These ancient Romans established trading routes throughout the Mediterranean region. While wheat and olive oil were among the major traded commodities, irises and other ornamental plants were also transported by Roman ships. Iris roots were carried throughout the Roman Empire, including those lands north of the Mediterranean. Irises soon flourished in Roman gardens throughout the empire, including those lands north of the sea.

Virgil, author of the *Aeneid,* the literary masterpiece of the Roman Empire, wrote about irises during the first century B.C. He noted the many variations of colors in his iris garden, shades of blues, violets and yellows, commenting that it was apt that the flower was named after the goddess of the rainbow.

A couple of centuries after the decline and fall of the Roman Empire in the fourth and fifth centuries A.D., Islamic invasions swept from northern Africa and the Middle East across Europe and into the Iberian Peninsula. In Spain, these invasions were known as the Moorish conquests. The Moors brought with them a rich heritage of plants, including cultivated plants, not the least of which were irises. They thrived in the walled gardens of the Moorish castles for many centuries. Most famous of these was the armed palace known as the Alhambra in Grenada, Spain.

The age of exploration began with Columbus's voyage in 1492. At that same time, his sponsors, Isabella and Ferdinand, drove the Moors from Spain. These two events, plus the consequential national friendships among Spain, Portugal and the Low Countries, including Holland, led to widespread distribution of the garden plants the Moors had brought. It was the talented plant growers and breeders of Holland who developed many of the early strains of English, Dutch, German and Spanish irises, ancestors of many of our own garden irises.

Irises were among the first ornamentals that came over on the ships with early settlers to the New World. They were on the plant lists of gardeners in Virginia as early as the 1600s. Even then, irises quickly became reliable mainstays of both home and public gardens throughout the young colonies. For many years, the only native iris the early colonists knew was the one they called blue flag. Later, they would discover others, including a dwarf iris from the Appalachian Mountains, the Louisiana iris and the Pacific Coast irises.

Sir Michael Foster (1836–1907) made many connections with plant collectors, missionaries and other friends throughout the world and thus was able to become the first person to seriously collect, grow and breed many iris species from the wild. Foster was the first in England to grow large irises from Asia Minor. These were naturally tetraploid irises (see Section VIII on the botany of irises to learn the value of tetraploidy) that became responsible for some of the major improvements in our garden irises. Foster kept detailed records and drawings of his irises. He defined many of the wild species and gave them specific names. His garden in Shelford, England, held the world's finest collection of iris species of that time.

One of Foster's friends was William Rickatson Dykes (1877–1925) who would write the then definitive book *The Genus Iris* in 1913. It was Foster's encouragement that set Dykes on his mission to study the entire genus. Dykes later wrote *A Handbook of Garden Irises* and *Irises*. He believed that as a botanist he should not only study irises in the herbaria of Europe and America, but should also study them in the wild and grow them before writing about them. His own garden began with donations from Foster and then grew as iris seeds and plants came in from all over the world.

Today, Dykes's work is somewhat outdated, yet it was the first of its kind in the iris world and offered a solid base of knowledge. The British Iris Society's highest honor for an iris, the Dykes Memorial Medal, was named in his honor. Today's taxonomists have new tools and greater knowledge to help them classify the irises. In Dykes's time, botanical classification was based primarily upon visible features such as seed shape, seedpod form and the structure of the tubular perianth that lies between the ovary and the flower. Today's botanists have access to chromosomal information and so can better tell the relationships among irises. There continue to be new irises discovered around the world and changes in classifications and the science of irises.

Foster and Dykes are important to the story of irises in American gardens. Their influence came through their introductions into the Anglo-American gardening world. In addition, up until the identification of DNA and consequent explosion of scientific technology beginning in the 1950s, Dykes's book *The Genus Iris* was the primary authority on the genus.

H. Meyer of Passaic, New Jersey, appears to be the first American iris hybridizer. Unfortunately, 'Carnot', his only known introduction, is lost. It must have been introduced before 1889 because Meyer mentions 'Carnot' in a list he published that year. The next known iris hybridizer in the United States was Eugene M. Dunphe of Elmwood, Massachusetts, a mechanic who also was an enthusiastic and skillful gardener. Dunphe bred a number of irises introduced at the turn of the century by J. K. Alexander, East Bridgeport, Massachusetts. Alexander's firm, founded in 1890, specialized in dahlias but he also bred some irises—which makes him the third known American iris hybridizer. It is sad that none of the irises hybridized by these three men are known to have survived.

A. Kennicott of Carbondale, Illinois, seems to be the fourth iris hybridizer of America. His iris cultivar, 'Fairy', was introduced in 1905 by William A. Peterson, Chicago, after Kennicott's death at age twenty. 'Fairy' is the oldest American hybrid known to survive to the present day. Peterson, a commercial nurseryman from 1903 to 1925, specialized in peonies. He introduced his pallida hybrid, 'Gertrude', in 1907 and it is still grown today.

The five men described above were all amateur breeders. Following them was America's great iris breeder, Bertrand Farr, whose life's work resulted in a quantity and quality of iris breeding that matched those of the great European hybridizers. He was the first American of this stature. Farr's hybrids first appeared in 1909, but none of those have survived. Nonetheless, those 1909 hybrids are of major historical importance, very popular at that time and widely used by other hybridizers. The only surviving Farr iris that continues to be grown and is well loved for its beauty and performance is the elegant 'Quaker Lady'. Other surviving Farr hybrids are the very rare 'Iriquois', 'Juniata', and 'Wyomissing'. Some of Farr's later hybrids, including 'Mildred Presby' and 'Seminole', are still grown but it was for the 1909 hybrids that he is remembered.

The intertwining stories of humankind and irises are many, sometimes parallel, sometimes conflicting, but always significant for those who love these beautiful flowers.

THE HISTORIC IRIS PRESERVATION SOCIETY

The original Historic Iris Preservation Society (HIPS) began at the 1986 American Iris Society convention in San Jose, California, when a group of irisarians organized under the leadership of temporarily appointed officers to preserve older iris cultivars. In 1988 at the AIS convention in Oklahoma City, they appointed a newsletter editor and published the first issue of *ROOTS*, the journal of the Historical Iris Preservation Society, that fall. The name of the group officially changed from "Historical" to "Historic" in 1989.

HIPS recognized the need for keeping track of ancestral irises. Too often, plant history is clouded by inaccurate records and the general failure of gardeners to keep good records. Most gardening catalogs emphasize new varieties. In many specialties of horticulture, new varieties keep coming out by the dozens every year. Iris breeders introduce hundreds of new irises annually. Soon there is not enough room for the new varieties in the catalogs and often in gardens, unless some of the older ones are dropped. That's how the old favorites disappear.

In 1989, HIPS began developing a database of historic irises, including irises introduced over thirty years ago, that soon numbered over 4,000. Many members have listed their irises in the database. Now, when someone is seeking an old historic iris, he or she can contact the HIPS source chairman, who will make a search for commercial and data bank sources. In addition, searches for historic iris sources, as well as information, take place through the HIPS biennial publication *ROOTS*. Experts will help identify unknown irises.

Iris latifolia, *the English iris, is actually native to Ibena. (Another woodcut version of this species from an old herbal; see also page 7).*

The historic iris 'Peacock's Eye', from the Probst Garden, Kirkwood, Missouri. (Photograph by Riley Probst.)

Ann Lowe, a past president and founder as well as first editor of *ROOTS,* said that the Historic Iris Preservation Society is dedicated to locating, recording, preserving and distributing antique iris cultivars. The group aims to educate the public and its members about antique irises and their historical significance in the development of present-day hybrid irises. They are conserving the antique iris gene pool to further present-day hybridization, and are compiling and publishing data on the location and availability of antique irises.

Dedicated HIPS members not only want to locate and identify these old irises, they also want to spread them around. They want to get historic irises into display gardens everywhere. HIPS provides a common thread that links together all the different sections of the American Iris Society. HIPS members have linked up with the other iris sections in their efforts to assist with the coordination and development of iris conservation programs.

Old iris catalogs are reference tools in identifying antique irises but, like all catalogs, they are known for their hyperbole, so photographs often are more valuable than descriptions. Points of identification include the rhizome, foliage, stem, bud and flower. Often, obscure characteristics such as purple-based foliage are critical to identification.

The challenge is overwhelming when you realize that there probably are over 50,000 named varieties of iris over thirty years old. Each year, another five hundred to seven hundred varieties join the ranks of historic iris.

The HIPS database has discovered some interesting things. The same old varieties keep showing up in many gardens. The age of the five most commonly found irises is astounding. They are 'Honorable' (1840), 'Wabash' (1936), 'Mme. Chereau' (1844), 'Rameses' (1929) and 'Dauntless' (1929).

Old irises are often seen in places other than old gardens—along back roads, in cemeteries, along fences, by mailboxes and by driveways. They soften the harsh lines of boundaries, add bright spots of color and texture to sometimes drab spots, and are always much more attractive than the usual collections of grasses and weeds.

In 1870, Edward Sprague Rand Jr. wrote in *Seventy Five Popular Flowers:*

> The different species of Iris are among the most showy of hardy perennials. No special culture is required, as the greater proportion grow freely in any garden soil and bloom well year after year. They are all very hardy, increase rapidly, flower freely, and are admirable

The historic iris 'Wabash' dates back to 1936, shown here in a Missouri garden. (Photograph by Riley Probst.)

bordering for the spring garden. By hybridization have arisen the host of varieties which we find in gardens, many of which present striking combinations of color, and are very beautiful. It is rare to find a genus where all its members are so showy and worthy of cultivation. For beauty and variety, we know of no family excelling the iris.

Anne Lowe has noted that reliability, hardiness and ease of cultivation in irises seem not as predictable in many of our contemporary hybrids. She strongly feels the need to facilitate the development of irises that will again

The historic iris 'Pinnacle', shown here in an Oklahoma garden. (Photograph by Jim Morris.)

meet some or all of the criteria outlined in 1870 by Rand. Some of the older cultivars that have survived the winnowing of time might furnish genes to help increase the hardiness of irises of the future. Present-day hybridizers would be wise to utilize some of these wonderful old irises. A look at the genetic background of some of the more successful irises tends to illustrate why they have remained at the top of the popularity polls. Call it hardy ancestors, good genes or careful selection—the fact remains that certain irises survive and perform consistently in large areas of the world.

For gardeners who decide to grow historic irises, Anne Lowe has some sound advice. When some of her recently acquired oldies bloomed for the first time in her garden, she found a number of misidentifications. Some were so obviously wrong that spotting them was automatic. However, she wonders just how many others that she doesn't know well enough to question may be masquerading under an alias. She has begun to play by the following rules: (1) Beware of antique irises purchased at local sales—they are often not as advertised. (2) Know from whose garden they came before you buy at an auction or sale. (3) Try to get at least two rhizomes from different sources of any iris whose identification is suspect—or even if it isn't, if the variety is very old or very rare.

SECTION II

Irises in American Gardens

THE ROLE OF IRISES
IN OUR GARDENS

The magic of irises in our gardens lies in their singular beauty, their linear quality and the ease with which they can be grown. The glory of the flowers and the brilliances and subtleties of their many colors endear the plants to gardeners. Irises make any garden more handsome and effective. Few perennials bring as much reliable color to garden beds and borders. Few are so adaptable to a wide range of soil and environmental conditions. Irises are major players in our gardens for good reason.

Irises have grown in American gardens since the earliest of times and probably came to the Colony of Virginia with Englishwomen who arrived in 1619. The Persian iris is in the old plant list for the governor's garden when Williamsburg was first planned in the seventeenth century. The bearded irises from Europe, the Middle East and North Africa, commonly called the German irises, crossed the Atlantic and were welcome introductions to American gardens wherever the colonists settled. The long congruent history of irises with humankind adds to the appeal of these old favorites of the perennial world.

Gardeners loved the ease with which they could grow irises, in addition to the beauty of the flowers. Apparently, the so-called German irises, a common name for the bearded hybrid irises that come in sizes from dwarf to tall, proved so popular that they became mainstays of American gardens in the earliest days of settlement. Incidentally, they do not come originally from Germany, as you will discover in this book. These bearded irises remain the most popular irises of all. Even now, when many species of both beardless and

Iris reticulata is a well-known member of the reticulated iris group native to Turkey, Iraq and Iran.

Spring is a colorful affair in the Goodman Iris Garden at the Missouri Botanical Garden. (Photograph by Barbara Perry Lawton.)

Japanese irises grace the edge of the lake in the Japanese Garden at the Missouri Botanical Garden. (Photograph by Barbara Perry Lawton.)

bearded irises are available, a mention of the iris plant brings to just about every gardener's mind the ones known as German bearded irises.

The roles that irises play in American gardens have grown to new heights with the full palette of species and varieties that is now available in both bearded and beardless groups. There has been an explosion of new varieties of irises during the past few decades. There are thousands from which you can choose.

From the earliest blooms of *Iris reticulata* to the fall flowers of the reblooming or remontant irises, the genus *Iris* covers the full growing season of the temperate zone. The remontant bearded irises have brought new meaning to the seasonal range of blooming irises. Soon we will have increasing numbers of reblooming irises from the beardless varieties. Already there are some reliable Siberian and Japanese reblooming irises.

Irises range in size from tiny dwarfs only a few inches tall to giants that grow to over 4 feet in height, their blooms carried like crowns above the foliage. Therefore, taller cultivars of irises serve as background plants in perennial borders while the smaller varieties serve well as edgings along the front edges of ornamental beds. There are all sizes in between the dwarfs and the giants, making it possible to find the exact sizes you may need for special situations.

In form, irises range all the way from the single-stemmed grace of the bulbous Dutch iris to the well-known spear sheaves of the bearded irises to the thick clumps of the Siberian irises. Again, there are all of the gradations of form in between these as well. That means that you can find an iris to fill just about any design need you might have in planning new beds and borders. In the case of the Japanese and Louisiana irises, you also can fringe a water area, a pool or stream, with these fine beauties.

As to flower form, again the range is wide. The standard petals may be upright or spreading. The falls may point downward or spread out like a saucer. The falls may have beards, crests, or neither. The size of the flowers may be miniature or larger than a tea saucer. Some iris flowers are heavily ruffled while others have no ruffles at all. The variety of flower forms is wide indeed, offering something for every taste.

When it comes to color and patterns of color, the genus *Iris* is hard to beat. The flowers, named for the Greek goddess of the rainbow, fulfill the promise of that name better each year as both professional and amateur iris breeders come up with new variations on the theme. Colors in irises run from the whites through yellows and oranges to pinks to blues, lavenders, purples and purple-reds. Pure geranium red is the only color that is not in the iris palette. There are the palest of pastels and the most robust rich shades imaginable. There are bicolored, spotted, blotched and speckled iris flowers. Some iris flowers have standards and falls of different colors. It is difficult to think of a color or color combination that you can't find among the irises.

The wide range of form, size, flowering season and color in irises combines with their environmental tolerances to make them plants for every garden in the temperate zone. The different irises can and do play many roles in American gardens—in rock gardens, alpine houses, woodlands, perennial borders, mixed ornamental beds, containers and water gardens. Some of the irises will make bold statements as accents if carefully placed. Imagine a large vigorous clump of Siberian irises placed just outside the junction of patio and home. Or a mass of crested irises on the outside of a bend in a woodland garden.

As American gardeners learn more about some of the less-used irises such as the spuria, Louisiana, Japanese and Siberian irises, their appreciation and use of irises in their garden designs will grow. Some of the more adventurous will even discover some of the many species irises that are captivating so many American Iris Society members.

As to site requirements for irises, they range from full sun and well-drained soil for the bearded irises to damp soil or even water sites for the yellow flag (*Iris pseudacorus*) and the Japanese iris (*I. ensata*). The bulbous Dutch, Spanish and English irises; the Pacific Coast iris species and hybrids; and Siberian irises (*I. sibirica*) will thrive in soil that is slightly damper than that in beds of bearded irises. The miniature bulbous irises (*I. reticulata* and *I. danfordii*) require excellent drainage such as that found in alpine or rock gardens.

Iris danfordii, *a bulbous iris, in very early spring in a Missouri garden. (Photograph by Barbara Perry Lawton.)*

31

DESIGN PRINCIPLES TO CONSIDER

Gardens are a blend of nature and human effort. The styles of gardening swing widely over the centuries from supremely egoistic formal gardens such as those seen at Versailles to the naturalistic wild gardens that are in the vanguard of today's garden designs in America. Irises fit well into both extremes and all degrees of garden design that fall in between the extremes. Your own tastes will probably fall somewhere in the middle. You might want to have one or two small formal areas in your garden while other main gardening areas are freewheeling designs featuring native plants.

Through observation of public and private gardens that you admire, you can train your eye to note pleasing combinations of plants and "hardscape" (the paved or otherwise nonearth parts of the garden). You can also learn to recognize incongruous elements in gardens, components that take away from the overall beauty of the garden. Whenever you see a garden, practice studying its design, learning to recognize its assets as well as those parts that are less successful.

In a beautiful garden, there is harmony among its parts. The design fits with its uses and role in the overall landscape. The individual plants and other design elements work well together. They fit together. They are pleasing. You feel comfortable in the garden. You like it! You may even want to adapt some of the elements to your own garden. It's a good idea to keep a small notebook and pencil with you so that you can jot down what particulars most impress you.

Remember that, as gardens mature over the years, the plants themselves make both subtle and bold changes to the original design. Young bearded

A magnificent landscape view of the Schreiner's Garden, Salem, Oregon.
(Photograph by Riley Probst.)

irises consisting of one or two fans of leaves grow into thick clumps crowned with many flowers in only a few years. Young trees grow taller and wider, changing the sun-shade ratio of garden spaces. In the spreading shade, a small clump of crested irises becomes an emerald swatch heavily painted with lavender blue each spring.

Today's gardens are often on a smaller scale than those of earlier times. While some of us may have the luxury—and obligations—of landed property, the majority of us have gardens that are easily measured in square feet rather than acres. Our gardens are often bound by property lines, the home, garage and, perhaps, storage shed, sandbox, swing set, picnic table, patio and other constructed items.

Designing gardens for small properties is challenging. There can be no meadows or sweeping swaths of naturalized plantings unless they are miniaturized. Plants for small-scale yards are easier to tend if they are easily controlled and not invasive. Paradoxically, one of the most important aspects of designing small properties is to keep the larger view in sight, to design with the total effect in mind.

I can't think of any twentieth-century landscape designer who has done a better job with small spaces than Thomas D. Church (1902–1978) of San Francisco. The confined spaces of many San Francisco properties inspired Church to develop garden designs that are elegant and roomy out of all proportion to their actual size. I had the good fortune to visit a number of Church-designed gardens, including his own, while in San Francisco in recent years. If ever there was a master of small spaces, it was Thomas Church. The designer faced with a small garden, he said, often wishes it were twice as large and so must use various techniques to create the illusion of space.

Like the seventeenth-century French design solution, trompe l'oeil, Church often used trellises, foreshortened paths and vistas to create the desired effect. In one case, Thomas was faced with a small yard that was bounded by a neighbor's garage. With vertical siding, some molding, an old door and a small brick terrace, he created the whimsical illusion of an entryway, transforming the ugly garage into an elegant image of a guesthouse.

Irises of all sorts fit right in with the design schemes for small properties. The larger Siberian irises, spurias and tall bearded types would work well in the farther reaches of flower beds while the miniatures and dwarf types are tidy focal points for niches and walkway beds. Use ground covers to integrate different plant groupings with one another.

The Morris garden of Ballwin, Missouri, in all its spring glory features many types of irises. (Photograph by Jim Morris.)

Although many iris aficionados plan their garden beds and borders to include just irises and often just certain kinds of irises, a more varied garden will be more pleasing to the eye for most of us. Iris collectors and breeders who are hard-pressed for space often must construct garden beds that are more for function than aesthetics. They need room for their parent plants and for the seedlings that are the result of their breeding experiments. Most of us can afford to mix other compatible plants in with our irises, plants that set off the irises with gentle contrasts in color, growing patterns and texture.

No matter what will be going into the gardens, the first thing to do is analyze the property from several angles. First, analyze what you want your garden to be, both aesthetically and functionally. This is the stage when the wisest thing to do is sit down and list on paper the things you expect your garden to do. If you have three small children, two dogs, a cat and rabbits, the

35

shape and style that your garden will take are far different from those of a couple with grown children and no pets who entertain adults a great deal.

Make a schematic diagram on paper noting everything you can about the area. Include desirable and undesirable views, sun and shade (both winter and summer), prevailing wind and the logical places to enter and exit. Note what trees, shrubs and herbaceous plants you should keep and which should be removed. Are there potential problems of flooding or water runoff that you should deal with early in the process of constructing the garden? Where are utilities and what are the existing zoning restrictions on fences, setbacks and so forth? What are the existing patterns of driveways, parking places and pathways? This may sound tedious but it is this diagram that is the basic analysis tool of all designers. It is at this stage that success or failure begins to appear to the experienced eye.

From the aesthetic point of view, do you want a vista, a series of cozy garden "rooms," a lawn area flanked by border beds or some other basic plan? Do you want to eliminate lawn and have gardens and ground covers throughout the property, both front and back? What kind of hardscape do you want to install? Walls, fences, paths, terracing, patios and other hardscaping will be critical to the garden's overview and also will help guide you in developing the garden beds, borders and accents. If you build walls or fences, think of them in relationship to the plants that will grow in front of them. Many ornamental plants including the irises, especially the taller ones, make stronger impressions when they are in front of an appropriate background.

We all spend a great deal of time within our homes. Therefore, when developing a landscape design, consider all aspects of that design from inside as well as outside. What will you see from the kitchen window? From the dining room window? From the living room window? And from the bedroom windows? These inside-to-outside aspects of garden design are too often forgotten. When placing major additions to the garden plan, have one person stand inside and signal from that point of view where the plants should go. Then double-check the site from other vantage points before planting.

Don't ignore the entrance area. It is this space that will set the tone for the property as a whole. Visitors and family members alike get their first impression of your grounds from the entryway. An attractive solution to this design challenge is to bend the front walkway or path around into an entrance-area garden room that might be only 8 by 10 feet. Define the space with a post-and-rail fence flanked by gardens or a hedge bordered with ornamental beds. Place paving stones and a small bench within the space so that there is room for several people to chat on the way in or out of your home. Here is where you can set the theme for your garden. Iris fanciers should find a few impressive varieties and place them on the outside of the space, then echo them by placing other smaller irises within the space.

Consider all of your ideas in relationship to both automobile traffic and pedestrian traffic. If a busy street is alongside your property, surely you will want a multilayer sight and sound buffer between the yard and the street. This might be an irregular line of pines and spruces interlined with evergreen shrubs—hollies, yews or others of your choice.

Once the preliminary planning is complete and necessary hardscape installed, some people like to site their garden beds on paper using diagrams carefully scaled to the size of the property. Others prefer to plan in situ using stakes, string and other props to outline the areas and to indicate the places for major components. Either way is fine—the important thing is to plan ahead so that your gardens will be as near your ideal as possible.

If you are overwhelmed at the idea of designing your property, call in a landscape architect or a garden designer. A simple consultation may help you understand where to begin. These experts will do as much or as little as you wish them to. They will talk you through the design process or they can develop a full-sized blueprint of the property plans. In the off-season, during the cold months, they have more time to devote to your landscape plan.

You can choose to have an overall plan designed, then break it into parts that you or your contractors can accomplish over a period of two or more years. Discuss your budget first, including the limits to spending for various aspects of planning, construction and plant installation. Some landscape architects will consult, plan, subcontract, oversee and handle every detail from A to Z. Make sure that you agree as to what is expected of the designer or architect you choose.

Once the beds and borders are in place, spend a great deal of time, money and effort on soil preparation. This may not be a true design principle, but it surely is one of the most important factors of gardening. If your soil is not of good quality, your plants will not thrive and your garden will reach far less than its potential.

When using irises in your garden design, consider their form, growing pattern, height, flower color, foliage color and the overall impression of each variety you plan to use. Be sure to know the expected times of bloom so that you can blend colors in a beautiful fashion for each season. Consider these factors in relationship to the other ornamentals you plan to use. Keep in mind the linear quality of irises with their spear-shaped leaf blades. Use these linear strokes to contrast with ferny or fluffy foliage of other ornamentals. Plan for succession of bloom throughout the growing season. Use irises to complement or contrast with other flowering herbaceous plants from spring through fall.

Remember that gardens are three-dimensional. When planning the massed plantings of perennial borders, the comparative heights of the plants are as important as their blooming times, structure, texture and colors. As a rule, place the tallest plants at the rear of a view, at the back of a border. But if you plant a lacy-foliage plant such as coral bells (*Heuchera* spp.) or Russian sage (*Perovskia*), it could be in front of plants of equal or lesser height in order to provide a veiled view. Russian sage planted in front of Siberian irises is effective for certain situations. There are other combinations that will work equally well. I once saw a patio that was several feet above the rest of the lawn and garden. Coral bells planted at the edge of the patio's ornamental border provided a lacy view of iris beds in the lower garden that was original and highly effective.

In America in the 1990s, the majority of gardeners want their gardens and homes to serve as sanctuaries from the stresses of the busy world. Those with a special love such as the "irisarian" has are lucky to have a special focus in their gardens, a favorite theme around which to build their own special sanctuaries. The garden sanctuary offers a place for contemplation, a place for pleasure.

To provide that spatial impact, your garden design should not be insistent with sharp edges and bright colors. The design should include space that provides solitude, privacy and security. Underline the sense of peace through the use of recessive cool colors. Develop areas of subdued light and soften the sound of the outer world with water features, a fountain or stream. Place moisture-loving irises as if they grew there naturally along the edges of water features.

Finally, remember that in garden design, the most important thing of all is to please yourself. This is your garden and no one else's. You are the only one you have to please. Therefore, if you break some of the rules of design, do it with panache. Think of yourself as a style maker, not a design sheep.

The Cortell-Wheeler Garden of Sacramento, California, shows how irises are used successfully in combination with other ornamentals in garden borders. (Photograph by Jim Morris.)

The Bearded Irises

TALL BEARDED IRISES

Irises play a spectacular role in spring's glorious celebration. In the eyes of many gardeners, the rainbow of tall bearded irises is the most spectacular show of the season. Not only do these irises come in colors that range from whites through almost-reds, yellows, oranges, pinks, blues and lavenders to almost black, they also come in many exquisite combinations and patterns of colors. These are the best known of the eupogon or true bearded irises.

HISTORY

These are the irises of your grandmother's garden, the ones that have been called German irises or flags. It was Carolus Linnaeus, the eighteenth century Swedish botanist, who assigned the binomial scientific name *Iris germanica* to the tall bearded irises. Linnaeus published *Species Plantarum*, his tome on botanical taxonomy, in 1753. This spelled out the system of binomial nomenclature that we use today. But Linnaeus erred on *Iris germanica*, the sample of which may have been sent from a German garden. The plant does not grow wild in Germany and, in fact, *Iris x germanica* is not a species but rather is probably a natural hybrid of intermediate height.

All of the ancestors of the bearded irises came from central, southern and eastern Europe and the Near East. Brian Mathew, a British world expert on the taxonomy of irises and author of *The Iris*, admits that the true original distribution of tall bearded irises is unknown and has concluded that they are almost certainly either natives of the Mediterranean region or hybrids of some species that occur there. He lists a number of what he calls "germanica-like plants."

Iris germanica is the best known of the old tall bearded irises.

'Dance Step', a tall bearded iris, is shown here in the Missouri Botanical Garden. (Photograph by Riley Probst.)

Tall bearded irises (TB) have played the starring role of the family Iridaceae for so long that detailed origins of this favorite perennial are shrouded with the mists of time. Quite probably, many of the iris species crosses took place naturally because of the proximity of the plants, and it's possible that early plantsmen were breeding irises many centuries ago. It is quite likely that early iris breeding was the process of selecting desirable irises from crosses made by bees rather than the modern human-made pollinations.

Most taxonomic botanists believe that modern bearded irises are the result of interbreeding among about fourteen wild iris species, including *albertii, cypriana, gatesii, kashmiriana, mesopotamica, pallida, trojana* and *variegata* (see section VIII, "The Botany of Irises"). Since the variations in size increased with these breedings, the bearded irises have been split into six different groups, based on plant size and growth habit as described under median irises in chapter 9.

CHARACTERISTICS

The leaves of tall bearded irises are sword-shaped, up to a foot and a half in length, and about an inch and a half wide. The surface of the grayish green leaves is glaucous, that is, it has a waxy coating that easily rubs off. The roots of bearded irises are fleshy, modified plant stems called rhizomes that store nutrients. The flowers, one or more on each stem, have perianths of six segments. The bearded irises also are called pogon irises, from *pogon,* the Greek word for beard.

The beard is the furry strip that runs longitudinally along the center of the falls, the three lower petals of the flower that actually are sepals. Iris beards, made up of many short hairs, serve to aid pollination by brushing pollen grains from visiting insects. The inner three segments, called standards, are usually erect and arching while the outer three segments, called falls, are often flaring or falling.

Tall bearded irises are in the horticultural grouping that grows to a height of more than 27 inches. They have branched flower stalks with multiple blooms, each on its own branch. These, the largest of the bearded irises, bloom later than the smaller bearded irises. In fact, you can safely assume that bearded irises will bloom each spring in most temperate zones in the same order as their heights. That is, the shorter varieties bloom first and the taller ones bloom later. In England and some parts of California, the intermediate bearded irises sometimes bloom before the miniature dwarf bearded irises and standard dwarf bearded irises. Shortest of all and earliest to bloom are the miniature dwarf bearded irises described in chapter 10.

Over the years, iris breeders have added many colors and color patterns to tall bearded irises. They also have changed the forms of the flowers and their substance. Some experts have estimated that well over half of the iris varieties offered for sale by commercial growers have originated in the past ten years. It is interesting to note that most iris breeders are skilled amateurs who consider their breeding trials an avocation rather than an occupation—that is not the case with other plants such as roses where most breeders are professionals on the staffs of horticultural organizations.

Today's irises remain in bloom for two weeks or more and many are both flared and ruffled. Some are what is called laced, with fringy edges to the standards and falls. The skimpy, droopy falls of earlier irises have become arched, more flared, well formed and broad in newer varieties, so broad that they almost overlap. The standards are of better substance in newer varieties, with sturdy midribs and full, rounded form. You can tell the substance of iris flowers by gently feeling the undersides of the falls. While some feel like tissue, others with good substance feel almost leathery.

Contemporary judging standards for irises stress performance and substance as well as aesthetics and so are valuable for those who merely want to grow irises. Each leaf of the foliage should be crisp, erect and of sufficient width, according to the judges' standards. The plant should thrive under good cultural conditions and remain vigorous without pampering.

Each plant should produce enough flowers to avoid a sparse look and also should produce enough increases in rhizomes to ensure bloom the following season. Branching of the flower stems in today's varieties displays the flowers in such a way that they don't interfere with each other and are evenly arranged on the top two-thirds of the stalk. A modified candelabrum is the best choice, with at least two branches plus the terminal buds on each flower stalk.

The tall bearded iris flower should be large and individually attractive, free from discordant or muddy colors. The beard color often contributes greatly to the beauty of the flower, either matching or contrasting with the flower. The beard should be generous and full, not scraggly or sparse. Color that fades is a liability to an otherwise beautiful iris flower.

In summary, an iris flower is considered of good quality when the falls are broad and gracefully flared. There should be no coarse markings (haft

Tall bearded iris, 'Hot Rhythm' in the Probst garden in Kirkwood, Missouri. (Photograph by Barbara Perry Lawton.)

marks) near the bases of the falls, but haft marks of pleasing color are acceptable. The standards should curve toward each other at the top of the flower. Standards and falls should be in good proportion to each other, and the flowers in good proportion to the plant.

The terms for different color patterns are confusing for the new irisarian but worth learning since they describe so well the variety of combinations. "Selfs" have flowers with standards and falls of the same color. "Amoenas" are bicolored bearded irises with white standards and falls of a different color. "Bicolors" have standards and falls of different colors. "Bitones" are irises with standards and falls of different shades of the same color. "Neglectas" have flowers that are blue or violet bitones. "Variegatas" are bicolored irises with yellow standards and falls of a different color—red, brown or purple. "Plicatas" have flowers with white, yellow, peach or pink ground color and a pattern of stitched or dotted edges in another color. "Blends" have flowers with both blue or purple and yellow or pink pigments. "Halos" have falls and sometimes standards outlined with a band of a lighter or different color.

Finally, there are the luminatas, probably related genetically to the plicatas, which are known for the absence of anthocyanin coloring in the heart and hafts of the iris flower. Anthocyanins are water-soluble pigments that impart to iris flowers colors of blue to purple. New breakthroughs occur regularly in iris breeding. For instance, the introduction of purple-stemmed bearded irises is expected in about 1998. This latest hybridizing breakthrough was undergoing seedling trials and evaluations in 1995.

CULTURE OF TALL BEARDED IRISES

Undoubtedly, one of the major reasons for the centuries-old popularity of the bearded irises is their ability to thrive under a variety of environmental conditions. Although the ideal soil for these irises would be 6.8, nearly neutral, they will grow quite successfully in soils with a pH range of 6.0 to 8.0, from mildly acid to somewhat alkaline. Neutral on the pH scale is 7.0 while anything below that is acid and anything above 7.0 is basic or alkaline.

If your soil is in the acid range with a pH of below 6.0, mix garden lime (ground dolomitic limestone) into the soil at the rate indicated on the container. To raise soil pH from 5.0 to 6.5 will take between 8 and 15 pounds of lime per 100 square feet, depending upon the soil type—less for sandy loam than for clay loam. If your soil is too alkaline with a pH of over 8.0, you can

44

lower it to the desired level by mixing aluminum sulfate, ferrous sulfate or soil sulfur into the soil at a rate of 2 pounds per 100 square feet. Wait two weeks, then test the soil again. Repeat if necessary.

A sunny site and medium fertility are requirements for top bloom production. Make sure that tall bearded irises get at least a half day of sun. Best performance will be in full sun. In extremely hot climates, some shade late in the day will be beneficial. Bearded irises tend not to thrive in the hot humid southern state of Florida and along the Gulf Coast where warm rainy summers are usual. They tend to do well in the drier regions of the southern states, USDA Zones 8–10 in Texas, Arizona and California. Of all the irises, the tall bearded varieties will be the most commonly found in gardens throughout our country.

Although bearded irises will grow well in a wide variety of soil types, they will perform to the greatest potential in soils that are classed as loam or clay loam. The major cultural requirement for soils in which you wish to grow bearded irises is good drainage. If your soil falls outside of these categories, it will pay to amend it with organic matter. For best results in improving the structure of extremely sandy or clay soil, cultivate 3–4 inches of compost, well-rotted manure or a good quality of peat moss into the soil to a depth of 12 to 15 inches two to three weeks before planting irises.

Those who live in areas where deluges of rain occur periodically, with as much as 2 to 4 or more inches of rain falling in one storm, would be well advised to consider growing tall bearded irises in raised beds. Avoid planting on slopes where rains can pile up silt and soil against iris rhizomes and even cover them. Those rhizomes will be most healthy if they are fully exposed to sun and air. Some experts recommend a light covering of soil in extremely cold climates while others stick with the recommendation to leave the rhizomes exposed to sun and air, no matter how cold the winter weather.

Climates where winter contrasts can range from 20 to 70 degrees F in a single twenty-four-hour period can be tough on irises. There are irises that do not go completely dormant or do not remain dormant during winter months—they can be grown most successfully in regions with mild climates. They probably would be lost in climates with harsh freeze-thaw cycles. Check with area irisarians, botanical gardens, nurseries and other experts before choosing TB varieties. Rogue out those that do not perform well in your garden. There are plenty of cultivars that will thrive, so why waste time on varieties

A close-up of the tall bearded iris 'Hot Rhythm' is shown here in a Missouri garden. (Photograph by Barbara Perry Lawton.)

that act wimpy in your particular region? A light mulch of loose straw also will protect tall bearded irises during snowless winters.

Clearly, it pays to have your soil analyzed if you want to have vigorous irises. If there is any doubt in your mind about the quality of the soil, contact your state university cooperative extension service and arrange to have a soil test. Regions with rainfall that averages less than 25 inches per year also will want the soil tested for soluble salts. If you garden in an area noted for either acid or alkaline soil, plan to have the pH tested every year or two. Although the costs of testing kits for nutrient levels are often more than you would spend on having the soil tested professionally, there are reliable inexpensive pH testing kits.

Cooperative extension agents will provide information on how to take soil samples and prepare them as well as where to take or send the sample. The cost of soil tests, usually plus or minus $15, is small compared to the benefit gained. When your soil test comes back, the report will include the amounts of various amendments that may be needed in order to have good soil for irises. Soil science is a complicated business but, since good soil is the basis for any successful garden, it will pay off in healthy vigorous plants to invest a considerable amount of effort in your garden soil.

Obviously, fertilizer recommendations will depend upon the specifics of your soil, but some good general materials are super phosphate and fertilizers with the 6-10-10 formulation. In general, avoid formulations that are high in nitrogen; these may actually encourage rhizome rot. Plan to make a light application of fertilizer in early spring before the bloom season and another light application about four weeks after irises flower.

Knowing the growing patterns of bearded irises explains why July and August are the months of choice for planting these irises in cooler climates and through late fall in warmer climates. From early spring until after the flowers appear, the plants' major growth is aboveground. The nutrients stored in the rhizomes are used for the growth of leaves, flower stalks, buds and flowers. Once the bloom period is past, plant growth during the next six to eight weeks concentrates on underground growth, on the development of increase buds that will become new rhizomes and on the development of new flower stalk buds for next year's growing season. At the same time, the plants are storing nutrients for next year's growth.

At the end of this underground growth period, the bearded irises are mature and, with the exception of the reblooming varieties that continue to grow throughout the warm season, will have a period of semidormancy. This is the best time to transplant them, when the rhizome is fully developed and while they are in their late-summer semidormant state. Plant at this time and the rhizomes will initiate new root growth in moist soil until hard frost. It is important that the roots of recently planted irises have an opportunity to become well established before the end of the growing season. Allowing the rhizomes to thoroughly dry out for several days or even a week will dry and callus the cut surfaces and diminish the chance of fungal diseases. A light dusting of horticultural sulfur also is a fungal deterrent.

If you order rhizomes from a commercial grower or you buy them locally, plan to have the bed ready for planting ahead of time. If the new irises have not already been cut back, lop off the leaf fans by at least half in order to prevent water loss while the plants are getting reestablished and making new root growth.

Dig a wide, shallow planting hole with a mound of soil in the middle. Set the rhizome on the mound and spread the roots out around it. Set the rhizomes with the fans facing the outer edge of the bed so that future growth will not result in a crowded mass of rhizomes. Fill with soil, making sure that the rhizome is at the soil surface and just barely exposed. In very light soils and in very hot climates, experts recommend covering the rhizomes with about an inch of soil. Water well, then water regularly if the soil is dry. Riley Probst of Kirkwood, Missouri, a hybridizer of tall bearded irises and recently regional vice president of the American Iris Society, warns that after tall bearded iris clumps are established, beware of overwatering. You should get some bloom the following spring, then maximum bloom the next year.

General care of garden irises includes thinning or dividing the plants every three to five years, depending on how crowded the plants are. See section VII, "Propagating Irises," for details and how-tos. Trim any injured, damaged or diseased foliage but leave the healthy green foliage undisturbed. Keep iris beds free of weeds and debris so that the tops of the rhizomes can bask in the summer sun. After the plants flower, cut or snap the bloom stems off close to the ground. Some irisarians mulch with an inch-thick layer of pine needles to keep down weeds, but be sure that the mulch does not touch or cover the rhizomes.

MEDIAN IRISES

The group of bearded irises that are intermediate in size between the dwarf species, their derivatives, and the tall bearded hybrids are called median irises. Jim Morris of Ballwin, Missouri, an iris enthusiast and president of the Median Iris Society, recommends the medians as a diverse and delightful group of irises that are most useful in extending the bloom season. They add new dimensions to the perennial border and deserve a place in everyone's garden. Jim notes that the median irises spawned a whole new interest in smaller irises in the late 1950s. This resulted in the formation of the Median Iris Society as a section of the American Iris Society (AIS).

The Median Iris Society, established in 1957, was the first specialized section of the American Iris Society. The four subgroups are standard dwarf bearded irises, intermediate bearded irises, miniature tall bearded irises and border bearded irises. Thus the term "median" refers to all of the bearded irises except the tall bearded irises and the miniature dwarf bearded irises. The arils and arilbred irises are a different breed of cat altogether, as you will discover in chapter 13.

Before the 1950s, there were small iris varieties that were mostly diploids, that is, they have 16 chromosomes, the original number of chromosomes for the species. Another expression used for diploids is "2n," with half of the chromosomes coming from each parent. These early small irises were derived primarily from *Iris lutescens* (formerly *I. chamaeiris*), a native of dry sites in Spain, southern France and Italy.

Later, the dramatic influence in the development of standard dwarf bearded irises (SDBs) and intermediate bearded irises (IBs) was from 32-

The standard dwarf bearded iris 'Pele' is shown here in a Washington State garden. This iris was named after the Hawaiian goddess of the volcano. (Photograph by Jim Morris.)

chromosome tetraploid (having twice the normal number of chromosomes, or 4n chromosomes) seeds of *I. pumila.* Later a number of other species, mostly tetraploids, from eastern Europe, including *I. cengialtii,* were collected and included in the foundation stock of miniature tall bearded (MTB), standard dwarf bearded and intermediate bearded irises. The advantages of tetraploids with twice the usual number of chromosomes are increased vigor, increased substance and larger size.

There are increasing numbers of reblooming median irises that further extend their already long combined blooming season. Few breeding programs were carried out for reblooming medians prior to 1980. Since then, many top-quality cultivars have been introduced. Good remontant medians should rebloom consistently in Zone 5, which typically has 150 frost-free days. Top breeder Lloyd Zurbrigg recommends crossing *Iris pumila* on remontant tall bearded irises to get median rebloomers.

The median irises are all those that are shorter than the tall bearded irises and taller than the miniature dwarf bearded irises, therefore all those that are "median" in height and bloom season. The Dwarf Iris Society section of AIS includes the miniature dwarf bearded irises—they are not part of the median iris group. The tall bearded irises, still the best known and most popular iris type, are covered under the auspices of the American Iris Society.

These divisions and sections of AIS are based upon the heights of the bloom stalks and were established as a horticultural convenience. I dwell on this classification system because it is a confusing aspect of irises. American Iris Society luminaries quickly realized that the Median Iris Society, with its four bearded iris subdivisions, must have well-defined standards and strict adherence to those standards. If you can learn which irises are included in the Median Iris Society and which ones are not, you will be well along on the road to understanding irises from a horticultural point of view.

STANDARD DWARF BEARDED IRISES

The standard dwarf bearded irises (SDBs) are the smallest but most vigorous of the median irises and the most numerous in registrations of named cultivars. When you consider the extreme hardiness and beauty of the SDBs, it is not surprising that they rank first in median registrations.

This class of irises, once called "Lilliputs," was first defined by the American Iris Society in 1959. The plants are 8 to 15 inches in height, measured from the ground to the top of flowers, with blooms that are 2 to 4 inches in width. Flower stems may be branched or unbranched and usually have two or more terminal buds. The leaves are erect and should be no taller than the height of the bloom stalk. These standards from the AIS *Handbook for Judges and Show Officials* are as dry as dirt, but necessary in describing this beautiful and useful group of irises.

These irises will cope with a wider range of environmental conditions than many other bearded irises. They will thrive in northern climates and withstand more wind than taller irises. SDBs can tolerate more shade than most bearded irises. In addition, they can tolerate more foot traffic than most irises and so are good choices for garden borders.

The blooming season for these irises begins after the peak of the flowering of miniature dwarf bearded irises, which are in their own Dwarf Iris Society section, and ends early in the intermediate bearded irises' bloom season. The blossoms, a bit taller than the foliage, cover the large cushiony clumps of foliage and come in all the colors found in other classes of iris. There are increasing numbers of remontant or reblooming SBDs. This quality makes them even more valuable to perennial gardens. For more about the reblooming irises, see chapter 12.

The foliage grows throughout most of the season, forming thick attractive mounds whose swordlike green leaves add an attractive texture to garden borders. The SDBs are an asset to gardens of all sorts, but work especially well in mixed beds of low-growing perennials and as border plantings in front of taller plants.

There has been substantial progress in the breeding of standard dwarf bearded irises over the past decade. SDBs have come about through the crossing of *Iris pumila* with tall bearded irises. With *I. pumila* in the genetic background of so many SDBs, it is not surprising that *pumila* spot patterns similar to that ancestor are common. Spots range from small to large and may be highly contrasting or have very little contrast. There also are outstanding varieties without spots, many with contrasting beards. There are some lovely plicata patterns with stitched or dotted petal edges in such combinations as the purple on white 'Royal Decree', burgundy on gold 'Firestorm' and brown on yellow 'Input'.

SDBs are also available in the color pattern called luminata, where the interiors of the flowers are pale in contrast to the dark blue or violet exterior ('Troubadour's Song'). This pattern is due to the absence of the bluish pigment anthocyanin in the hafts and heart of the flowers. There also are SDBs with color contrasts between the standards and falls. 'What Again' has wisteria blue standards and falls the color of golden straw.

This art work appears to be of an old spuria iris, perhaps Iris graminea.

New colors and patterns that are appearing in SDBs include better and darker oranges with red beards, pinks with blue beards, chartreuse yellow with red beards and pale blue standards with blue-green falls and red beards. Only the imagination can create standard dwarf bearded irises more astounding than those in reality. They also come in reverse amoenas, that is, flowers with colored standards and white falls, as well as amoenas with white standards and colored falls.

There is such a tremendous variety of colors and patterns among the standard dwarf bearded irises that extra study of catalogs is in order to decide how many kinds you can cram into your garden. Their variety, combined with their vigor and ease of care, make SDBs a star for most American gardens. Recent tallies of median iris catalogs by median expert Jim Morris indicate that there are more standard dwarf bearded irises listed than all three other median classes combined.

The intermediate bearded iris 'Tie Dyed Tyke', shown here in an Oregon garden. (Photograph by Jim Morris.)

INTERMEDIATE BEARDED IRISES

The intermediate bearded irises (IBs) are so named because both their height and their bloom season fall in between those of the standard dwarf bearded irises and the tall bearded irises. These median irises must be 16 to 27 inches tall with straight flower stalks that are branched and extend above the erect foliage. The flower stems usually have two branches and five buds on each stalk.

The flowers are 3 1/2 to 5 inches wide and bloom during the period between the bloom seasons of the standard dwarf and tall bearded irises. The intermediate bearded irises have the same height requirements as the border bearded irises (see below) but the blooming seasons are different—IBs must have peak bloom earlier than the TBs' blooming season. There is some variation in the bloom season, depending upon the variety's breeding and the size of the flowers, with the smaller ones blooming earlier.

The intermediate bearded iris class includes mostly hybrids that are crosses between tall bearded and standard dwarf irises, but some are the result of crosses between tall bearded irises and species such as *Iris aphylla* and *I. lutescens*. Breeders have used *I. aphylla* to improve IB fertility, branching and bud count. Although the IBs have strong hybrid vigor, the fertility of these 44-chromosome hybrids is greatly reduced because of their complex genetic structure. As a result, it is less likely that IBs can be crossed with each other to create new cultivars because so many are sterile.

These irises very much resemble their larger tall bearded cousins. They are of good substance and pleasing form, with falls that are flared and rounded and standards that are arched and closed, often with lace or ruffles. Intermediate irises come in the full range of colors and combinations that are found in tall bearded irises.

In the garden, the intermediate bearded irises fit, in both size and bloom time, in between the standard dwarf bearded and the tall bearded irises. Thus they are an integral part of the parade of irises that can provide bloom from early spring until the first hard frost. Their inherent vigor makes many of the IBs dependable rebloomers.

Some irisarians argue that these are the easiest to grow of all the bearded irises. They are dependable bloomers, vigorous, disease-resistant and very hardy. They can withstand high winds, sudden freezes and other sudden weather changes with little damage. They are also easy to work with in flower arranging.

Breeders have succeeded in improving the width, substance and quality of pink intermediate bearded irises, an example of which is 'Blushes'. 'I Bless' is a deep bitone, reblooming, daffodil yellow that is the result of a cross between an intermediate bearded iris and a border bearded iris. Breeders are learning how to check for the fertility of IBs so that they can use them as stepping-stones to improve standard dwarf bearded, tall bearded and other irises. Just over the horizon are new intermediate bearded irises that undoubtedly will astound even the most jaded gardener.

MINIATURE TALL BEARDED IRISES

The miniature tall bearded irises (MTBs) are also called table irises and have been bred for small gardens and floral designers. In size, MTBs are 16 to 25 inches tall with stalks that are 1/8 to 3/16 inch in diameter and flowers with a combined height and width of not more than 6 inches. The ideal height is 21 to 22 inches rather than the extremes of 16 and 25 inches.

An added attraction to the judging standards of this class is a pleasant fragrance that is important in miniature tall bearded irises. An unpleasant fragrance would make a seedling unacceptable because no one would want it in a table arrangement. The blooms of these irises rise well above the foliage. The flower form of MTBs is less ruffled and airier than the larger flowers of tall bearded irises, which gives these irises a look reminiscent of wildflowers. The bloom season is later than intermediate bearded irises and much the same as that of border bearded and tall bearded irises, around mid-May to mid-June

53

in northern states, but there also are early and late-late cultivars. The MTBs are generally the best branched of all classes of median irises.

The miniature tall bearded irises look very much like modern delicate versions of the old-fashioned tall bearded irises, the ones you still see in many old gardens. The plants are miniature versions of tall bearded irises and are different from the intermediate bearded and border bearded irises in that they are slighter smaller in both plant and flower, and thinner and more graceful, with well-branched, wiry stems.

Iris breeders are improving the flower form and broadening the range of colors of MTBs using older diploid species and newer tetraploid cultivars. While most of the current table irises derive from older diploid bearded irises, the background of the new pink MTBs is strictly tetraploid hybrids. Many species of smaller bearded irises are being used in MTB breeding programs, including a small red-violet–flowered one from Russia that promises to provide slim stems and reduce the size of larger irises.

Amoenas with their white standards and colored falls, plicatas with stitched or dotted edges on the petals, pale colors and bright colors—all can be found among the miniature tall bearded irises. The ideal iris for flower arranging, the MTBs also fit well into perennial beds and borders.

BORDER BEARDED IRISES

The median iris group known as border bearded irises (BBs) was designated a subclass of the tall bearded division by the American Iris Society in 1958. In the 1940s, iris breeders were noticing small versions among their tall bearded iris seedlings. Although they had little chance to compete with the larger bearded irises, they had an appeal of their own. They didn't overwhelm a mixed ornamental bed or border, didn't blow over in spring storms, and their smaller size made them easier to work with in flower arrangements.

The judging standards describe border bearded irises as having flower stalks 16 to 27 inches in height with flowers 4 to 5 inches in diameter. Flowers are borne on stiffly erect, branched stems and the leaves are erect and shorter than the flower stalks. These irises bloom at about the same time as tall bearded irises, bearing flowers that are smaller than those of the tall bearded irises but larger than those of the miniature tall bearded irises.

The early requirements for border bearded irises had no specifications for flower size, slimmer stems or narrower foliage. In the 1960s, however, a number of breeders analyzed the balance and proportions of BBs and

The miniature tall bearded iris 'Eversweet' captured in Sass Memorial Garden in Omaha, Nebraska. (Photograph by Jim Morris.)

54

presented a formula to *The Medianite,* the quarterly publication of the Median Society, in 1967. The recommendation was that the flower size (height plus diameter) for border bearded irises should be no more than 9 inches and that the stalk height should be roughly three times the flower size. At the same time, recommendations for foliage width and stem size were given. Although most breeders believe these are sensible suggestions, they have not been officially adopted into the judging standards of the AIS.

Vigor has proven to be a problem in growing BBs because some cultivars proved to be small only because they lacked the specific environment to reach their genetic potential. When provided with the right site, moisture and nutrients, some BBs grew to be tall bearded irises.

Border bearded iris breeders made great progress in the 1960s and 1970s. One of the earliest of the well-proportioned BBs was 'Crystal Bay', a derivation of the legendary 'Progenitor', a seedling of the tetraploid dwarf species *Iris reichenbachia.* This pointed the way toward using other tetraploid dwarf species to control size and growth habit as well as new flower patterns.

The breeding of border beardeds slackened during the 1970s, perhaps because this class of irises is so frustrating—a breeder might raise dozens of special crosses only to find that none fit within the BB size requirements. Toward the end of the decade, some significant achievements were made, including both color patterns and vigor. Breeders expect that soon border bearded irises will reproduce themselves reliably.

Iris species, including dwarf and larger versions of *Iris aphylla*—not always a dwarf species especially when used in border bearded iris breeding—*I. balkana* and *I. reichenbachii,* now are in the border bearded gene pool and adding their colors and patterns as well as their excellent proportions and small flower size to the breeding stock. As a result, today's breeders are able to raise large crops of border bearded irises in which the majority of young plants fit within the BB requirements.

Good contemporary border bearded irises should be in good proportion rather than merely a short stem with flowers the size of tall bearded iris blooms. The overall effect should be one of a compact daintiness that is distinctly different from the overall impression one gets from tall bearded irises. These plants will not need staking and their small flowers are excellent for flower arranging. Use border bearded irises to edge a sunny garden or, by definition, as a border.

The border bearded iris 'Faux Pas', shown here in the photographer's Missouri garden. (Photograph by Riley Probst.)

Miniature dwarf bearded iris 'Tooth Fairy', shown here in the Morris garden in Missouri. (Photograph by Riley Probst.)

MINIATURE DWARF
BEARDED IRISES

The Dwarf Iris Society is devoted to the small plants classed as miniature dwarf bearded irises (MDBs), plants that grow to 8 inches or less in height. The flowers reach only 2 to 8 inches in height. The pumila types of irises don't have proper stems, but rather flowers growing on extended perianth tubes. In iris flowers, the perianth is a collective word for the standards and falls. These are the tiniest of the bearded irises and also the earliest to bloom. The miniature dwarf bearded irises are beautiful and reliable choices for rock gardens or when planted in drifts to give a colorful carpetlike effect in early spring. Dainty and small, the MDBs are attractive in the very early spring when the tiresome winter is over and the iris clumps bear their bright little flowers.

HISTORY

The majority of miniature dwarf irises are descended from *Iris pumila* and *I. lutescens* (syn. *I. chamaeiris*). *I. lutescens* is native to dry rocky parts of southern Europe. Because of its great variety of colors—yellows, violets and occasionally white—*I. lutescens* has been known by many names. It even has been called, incorrectly, *I. pumila,* which causes further confusion. Indeed, the dwarf irises have commonly been called *pumila* irises for centuries.

In recent years, chromosome counts and cytogenetic studies have straightened out the relationships of these two major ancestors of MDBs. Some of the varieties originally considered to be pure *I. pumila* have turned out to be natural hybrids of *I. pumila* and *I. lutescens*. One of these is 'Atroviolacea', a famous cultivar known at least since the mid-1800s and often called the cem-

The miniature dwarf bearded iris 'Golden Eyelet', shown here in a Missouri garden. (Photograph by Barbara Perry Lawton.)

etery iris. This iris was carried across North America by early settlers and often used to cover graves. 'Azurea' and 'Coerulea', though not nearly as well known, have been cultivated at least since 1880.

I. pumila has served as a founding parent of three different iris classes since its arrival in the United States: the miniature dwarf bearded irises and also the standard dwarf bearded and intermediate bearded irises. The plant was originally brought to England by soldiers returning from the Crimean War, but it wasn't widely distributed there and was scarcely available in our country until the 1930s, when Robert Schreiner imported seeds from Romania and Vienna. From these early imports came three major cultivars, a violet blue 'Sulina', yellow 'Carpathia' and red 'Nana'.

In the 1940s, Schreiner sent some of his dwarf irises to Paul Cook, who was able to breed irises of a truer blue than previously known. It was Cook who submitted a dwarf iris rhizome to Walter Welch, the man appointed by the American Iris Society to head the new Dwarf Iris Committee. Welch organized the Dwarf Iris Society and thus began an important period for miniature dwarf bearded irises. Welch himself earned many honors for dwarf iris breeding.

CHARACTERISTICS

Miniature dwarf bearded irises bloom along with daffodils. They are 8 inches or under in height, although varieties registered with the AIS before 1976 may be up to 10 inches tall, yet still be classified as MDBs. The flower stems usually are unbranched and the flowers are 2 to 3 inches in diameter. These are the earliest to bloom of all the bearded irises. The flowers should flare, stand up above the foliage and be in good proportion to the plant as a whole.

The most important species in the genetic background of modern MDBs is *Iris pumila.* Miniature dwarf bearded irises of pure *I. pumila* background seem to be nearly a class by themselves. Most MDB varieties include one-half to three-quarters *I. pumila* parentage. The remainder of the genetic background of MDBs is often complex and comes from tetraploid tall or border bearded irises, the 40-chromosome species complex known as *I. lutescens,* and, increasingly, *I. aphylla.*

When growing MDBs, you should remember that they are extremely variable in color from year to year and from garden to garden. A given variety might have a sharp and clear *I. pumila* spot pattern in one year or in one garden and have an indistinct fuzzy pattern in the next. Dark irregular streaking or blotching may appear in cold, wet weather on varieties that are normally clear. This is particularly noticeable on light-colored flowers.

CULTURE

If there is any one single factor that will cause miniature dwarf irises to fail, it is poor drainage. These small irises must have well-draining soil. The slightest hint of sogginess can be enough to encourage rot. This is not surprising since some of their ancestors were originally collected on the rocky cliffs of eastern Europe and western Russia. Cold winters are another environmental need for dwarf irises; in fact, the colder the winter, the greater the numbers of flowers for most of these plants.

The MDBs with a high proportion of *pumila* in their genes do not transplant well. They seem to take a long time for new roots to develop. Their dislike for being moved is sometimes reflected by a whole clump collapsing and dying. Other MDBs that don't have *pumila* genes will transplant better.

Iris aphylla, *a bearded iris species native to central and eastern Europe.*

MDBs will grow in more shade than the bearded irises that bloom later in the season. Perhaps that is because they bloom before tree leaves emerge. Because of their shallow roots, MDBs tend to heave during freeze-thaw cycles. This is no problem where snow covers them but can be a nuisance when there are open winters with little or no snow. Once the ground is frozen, cover these small irises with a light mulch such as loose straw or hay. Beware of letting too much soil accumulate on top of the rhizomes, especially during spring and summer when the irises are growing strongly.

Keep beds of miniature dwarf bearded irises weeded. Not only will weeds rob the irises of nutrients in the soil, they may also shade the irises. Weed often and after rains have softened the soil to make the task far easier. When fertilizing, use a formulation or material that is high in phosphorus, the second number on fertilizer containers. Scratch the fertilizer into the soil around the plants.

Brian Mathew, botanist and international iris expert, notes that his *pumila*-derived dwarf irises thrive for a couple of years, then dwindle and disappear. He recommends growing them in raised beds with soil that is lime-rich and with nutrients that are not overly high in nitrogen. The lush growth that nitrogen-rich fertilizers encourage is highly susceptible to winter injury and loss.

'Pronghorn', a novelty horned bearded iris with pronounced horns and/or flounces, pictured here at the Missouri Botanical Garden. (Photograph by Riley Probst.)

NOVELTY BEARDED IRISES

What do you do when you find plants that don't fit into any known category? The American Iris Society solved this problem by creating the category called novelty bearded irises. This iris class includes such oddities as the beardless bearded iris. Also included are those irises whose flowers have odd forms such as horns, spoons or flounces.

As the quality of novelty bearded iris flowers and plants improves, this miscellaneous class of irises is becoming more popular. Growers and hybridizers, aware of the increasing interest in oddball irises, are keeping unusual plants that appear unexpectedly in their seedling beds and then striving to improve the quality of these novelty irises.

HISTORY

Back in the 1930s, some irises were observed in seedling fields that had curious bumps on the edges of the flower petals. The person who had hybridized them thought this had come about because of too much inbreeding. He considered these plants undesirable. However, there were other iris hybridizers who liked this trait and began breeding programs to emphasize and refine the bumps into what we know today as laced blooms. The extravagantly laced flowers of 'Grand Waltz' and 'Laced Cotton' were developed from those bumpy-petalled flowers of the 1930s.

Early in the twentieth century, flat bearded irises appeared with six bearded falls and no standards. Among the beardless irises, the flat form of the Japanese iris is a very popular type. Flat flower forms also occur in Louisiana and Siberian irises. Occasionally, a bearded iris has mutated into what is called a tulip-type, that is, it will have six standards and no falls. The tulip-type of iris flower usually has little or no beard.

CHARACTERISTICS

The judging standards for novelty irises are, as you might suspect, challenging. Iris judges are encouraged to make every effort to evaluate novelty irises intelligently rather than simply dismiss them as freaks. The rule of thumb is that the better the flower, the better the novelty iris. The flower must be beautiful even though it looks radically unlike an ordinary iris. In addition to unusual form, novelty irises should be of good quality and bud count, with firm stalks and vigorous growth habits.

Newcomers to this group of irises should note that herbicides containing glyphosate such as Roundup and Kleenup may cause strange aberrations in iris flowers. These, of course, would not breed true since they represent damage to the plant rather than genetic mutations. Herbicide damage may cause petals to have no pigment at their edges and the entire flower to have a strappy look. The flowers might be smaller or their parts oddly out of proportion. Always be very careful when using weed killers. Never apply them when it is windy.

There are multi-petalled novelty irises with flowers that display more than three standards and three falls. Yet the flowers should still have the basic outline of an iris flower. There are novelty irises with irregular color applications.

Unstable color genes may produce flowers with a contrasting pattern of two colors, one of them usually white. The pattern, which should not be confused with the plicata pattern that features a contrasting dotted pattern on the edges of flowers, may be quite varied but distinct. This haphazard color patterning is highly thought of in roses and camellias. The same genetic color pattern is fairly common in Japanese irises and is also known in the bearded iris classes, though less often.

'Joseph's Coat', an unregistered diploid miniature tall bearded iris, is the only iris thus far known to have what is called variable coloring. This iris cannot receive any AIS awards because it is not a registered and officially introduced variety. The color pattern of the flowers ranges from a yellow-and-red variegata type to an amoena type with white standards and violet falls.

The more the color varies on a given flower stalk, the better, according to admirers of this unusual cultivar.

Flat-shaped flowers are novelty irises with six falls arranged in a horizontal to downward arching pattern with six visible beards. Although there usually are no standards, flat-shaped iris flowers will occasionally have one standard. This novelty iris is especially effective when the petals are very wide. Flat-shaped novelties may have one or two partially normal flowers on the same stalk with the flat flowers, an inconsistency that is to be expected, but not desired. A good novelty iris should consistently display its novelty characteristics.

The flowers of iris plants with variegated foliage are seldom impressive, but the foliage can be in handsome combinations of green with white or green with yellow. *Iris pallida variegata,* with foliage striped in yellow and

The novelty iris 'Very Varied', which features broken color, an unusual flower variegation, captured in the Gayer Garden in rural Missouri. (Photograph by Riley Probst.)

63

green, and *I. pallida argentea,* with white and green-striped foliage, are the best-known varieties of this type of novelty iris. Breeders are working to develop tetraploid versions of variegated-foliage irises that will include the typical distinctive substance and vigor found in tetraploids.

The popular novelties known as horned, spooned and flounced irises all have projections that grow at the ends of the falls' beards. "Horn" is the term for a short, stubby protrusion of the beards. They should emphasize and add a kind of lilt to the line of the beard. "Spoon" refers to an elongated version of the projection that ends in a wider end, giving it a spoon effect. A "flounce" is a still larger projection at the end of the beard that grows in a wide, folded, sometimes canoe- or fan-shaped growth pattern. Protrusions and filaments that end in a spoon or flounce should be sprightly and graceful, adding a certain charm to the overall effect of the flower. These extensions should be in proportion to the flower and neither weigh down nor distort the form of the flower. They should also be consistent from flower to flower.

Since many novelty irises are the result of mutations, they do not always exhibit the mutant characteristics consistently. Ben R. Hager of Stockton, California, iris expert and breeder of novelty irises, notes in a 1984 *Bulletin of the American Iris Society* that "our tendency is to drool over the normally abnormal flowers that are fully flat and six-bearded and pretend the others will go away—which they actually do when we surreptitiously pick them and throw them away so nobody else will see them."

The better cultivars of novelty irises will display their particular characteristics with marked regularity. As time goes by, hybridizers are bound to succeed in breeding novelty iris varieties that have more consistent growth and flowering habits.

CULTURE

Grow novelty irises in the same way as you would the iris classes from which they have arisen. In other words, if the novelty comes from a line of tall bearded irises, then grow it just as you would the TBs. The same goes for any of the novelties—you need only know what the background of the plant is.

REBLOOMING OR REMONTANT IRISES

Visitors to iris gardens in the fall are curious, even astounded, when they see irises in bloom. Iris fanciers and gardeners in general are delighted to discover increasing numbers of reblooming or remontant irises. Through selection and breeding programs, iris breeders have greatly increased the number of irises that will bloom during more than one period of the year, thus expanding the potential enjoyment and appreciation of garden irises.

These days, some remontant irises will rebloom after the first spring flowers and every three to four weeks after that until the first hard freeze. That kind of reliable reblooming habit is the aim of every breeder of remontant irises. The blooming season for these irises often begins right after the peak of the flowering of miniature dwarf bearded irises.

HISTORY

Most of these rebloomers are tall bearded irises, a fact that is probably related to the great popularity of the bearded irises. They are also being discovered and developed in dwarf and border forms, and are increasingly available in the same full range of forms and color patterns as the tall bearded irises. There now are remontant irises that are ruffled and some that are laced in form. And there are varieties that are bicolored, including amoenas, variegatas and plicatas.

There are thousands of bearded iris cultivars with many new varieties being bred, named and registered every year. Now that gardeners and irisarians alike are reaching out beyond the bearded irises and learning more about

Iris biflora, *an obsolete name referring to an early reblooming iris.*

beardless and species irises, remontant irises of those types are showing up as well.

Iris breeders are spotting rebloomers among spuria, Japanese, Siberian and other irises. They are selecting them for breeding programs that will extend and repeat the blooming seasons for these irises as well. Now we can safely look ahead to a time when we will have not just a few, but many irises in bloom periodically or even regularly throughout the growing season.

The rebloomers, depending on their bloom schedules, are described as continuing, cyclical and repeat bloomers. Although the first mention of reblooming irises appeared as *Iris biflora* in John Gerard's 1597 *Herbal,* it wasn't until the past decade or so that rebloomers became more reliable and more aesthetically acceptable in garden circles. Reblooming irises first showed up on sales lists in the 1930s, but they were more curiosities than great irises.

CHARACTERISTICS

Until the 1980s, the remontant irises often competed poorly with the once-blooming types for a number of reasons. First, they didn't conform to the judging ideals. The proportions of bloom to plant or falls to standards often were out of whack and their colors often were lacking in beauty as well. In addition, the degree to which they would extend and repeat their blooming times was greatly dependent upon the climate and the growing season, both generally and specifically.

Fortunately, many dedicated hybridizers have been successful in breeding reblooming irises in many parts of the country. Thus there now are remontant irises for iris lovers throughout the United States. Since irises need warm weather and plenty of sun in order to rebloom, there are fewer rebloomers in northern regions. Those rebloomers that will succeed in northern states have a tendency to bloom earlier in the spring, because then they have enough time to develop new flowers before frost.

Many of the reblooming irises tend to develop many candelabrum-type flower stalks, something you don't see as much in the spring. One called 'Sky King' looks like any other tall bearded iris in the spring but then develops candelabra later in the season and may have as many as fifteen or sixteen flowers in bloom at once, a profusion of color. Some varieties are of good quality in their spring blooms, but not as fine in the fall.

The reblooming tall bearded iris, 'Happy New Year', shown in the Ann Probst Memorial Garden in Kirkwood, Missouri. (Photograph by Barbara Perry Lawton.)

The reblooming tall bearded iris 'St. Petersburg' in all its beauty, shown here at the Missouri Botanical Garden in late October. It is equally handsome in spring. (Photograph by Barbara Perry Lawton.)

The reblooming tall bearded iris 'Earl of Essex', shown here in the photographer's Missouri garden. (Photograph by Riley Probst.)

'Immortality' is one of the remontant irises that has earned an important place in the gardens of experts and amateurs alike. This spectacular white iris seems to flower continuously, beginning again in July. This variety increases rapidly and reliably reblooms in the fall except in regions with very cold winters. 'Immortality' won an Award of Merit from the American Iris Society in 1990, the only tall bearded rebloomer to date to do so. The previous year, in 1989, Dr. Lloyd Zurbrigg's handsome yellow remontant standard dwarf bearded 'Baby Blessed' won the AIS Cook-Douglas Medal—this is the highest honor an SDB iris has earned. These two award-winning remontant irises put the rebloomers on the map.

Lloyd Zurbrigg of Durham, North Carolina, an iris breeder and grower of four decades, bred 'Immortality' in 1982. It was voted tops in the 1993 Reblooming Symposium ballot. In fact, Zurbrigg, a former music professor, had a number of tall bearded irises ('Earl of Essex', 'Harvest of Memories', 'Jennifer Rebecca' and 'I Do') in the top nine of the Reblooming Symposium, and also the most popular rebloomer in the standard dwarf bearded section ('Baby Blessed') and in the intermediate bearded section ('I Bless').

The smaller the flowers, the greater the tendency for the plants to rebloom both longer and earlier, according to Ken Kremer, an iris hybridizer of Amberway Gardens in St. Louis, Missouri. For instance, the standard dwarfs will bloom very early in the spring and then may rebloom when the tall bearded irises first bloom in the spring.

The reblooming standard dwarfs may have a second cycle of bloom at the end of the tall beardeds' first cycle, along toward the last week in May or first week of June. They may rebloom again in September. Kremer notes that a cultivar called 'Jewel Baby' has rebloomed as many as five times in one season. A tall bearded iris that is enthusiastically remontant is 'Queen Dorothy', a blue plicata that blooms prolifically and grows like a weed.

In recent years, irisarians have been increasingly discovering reblooming irises that do not come under the bearded iris umbrella. These are in turn being hybridized so that the blooming season for irises begins to look as though it will go from very early spring until frost and include elegant beardless irises as well as our old favorites, the spectacular bearded irises.

Dr. Currier McEwen, an iris hybridizer and grower in Maine, has long noted a considerable difference in the reblooming patterns of beardless irises such as the Japanese and Siberian irises as compared to the reblooming bearded irises. While the bearded irises may take several months to begin a second bloom cycle, the beardless irises have shorter rest periods, often reblooming in as little as one to three weeks after the final flowers of the first bloom period.

McEwen and Bee Warburton, both internationally noted iris experts and hybridizers, have proposed that the term "repeat bloom" or "repeaters" be used for the reblooming Japanese and Siberian irises. McEwen has observed that the Japanese and Siberian irises fall into several categories pertaining to their habits of reblooming. First is the largest number that bloom but once each growing season. Second is the moderate number of those that may show repeat blooms in some years, but not in others—he calls these occasional repeaters.

Third is a small group that will dependably repeat bloom with bloom quality equal to the first blooms, so long as they are growing well. Fourth are a few that show dependable rebloom with better flower and stalk quality at the second bloom—better bud count, better branching, taller stalks. Finally, the fifth group includes a rare few valuable plants that continue to develop successive stalks for a longer period than the normal bloom season. McEwen considers this last category especially valuable in the case of Japanese irises.

CULTURE

Even the toughest of rebloomers will not reliably repeat their bloom in areas in USDA Zone 4, where winter temperatures can reach minus 30 degrees F. But growers have discovered that if an iris successfully reblooms in places like northern Illinois, Nebraska and other regions in Zone 5, it is likely to be as reliable in other areas of that zone as well as areas in warmer zones. Gardeners in colder regions may be able to identify warmer microclimates in their gardens where rebloomers can succeed. These microclimates often occur near buildings sheltered from winter winds, in the lee of brick or stone walls, on the south sides of structures, and similar sites.

If the temperature goes down to 28 degrees F while remontants are in bloom, the flowers will last but will look very much like tissue paper the next day. If the temperature goes down to 25 degrees, they are done for. If temperatures threaten to go into the 20s, pick all the flowers that afternoon. You may as well have some handsome bouquets to celebrate the season.

Rebloomers require a lot of water, more than you would dare give once-blooming irises for fear of encouraging rot. Water rebloomers heavily every week to ten days to saturate the soil. The reblooming irises will not get rot nearly as fast as regular irises because they take in more water from the soil to sustain their longer growing periods.

Since they produce flowers more than once each growing season, the remontant irises also need more nutrients than once-blooming irises. Kremer observes that they require about twice as much nutrient. He recommends alfalfa meal or pellets to sprinkle on the ground, making sure it does not come into direct contact with the rhizomes. Put alfalfa pellets a couple of inches apart.

Alfalfa is an old-time fertilizer that was used as a green manure by farmers and is enjoying a rebirth in popularity. Farmers would plant it, then plow it under at about 6 inches in height, let the ground set for a few weeks, then plant the crops. Alfalfa, a natural organic fertilizer that will not burn the plants, contains nitrogen, phosphorus and potassium as well as trace elements that are important for growth and vigor. It enriches the soil with nutrients at the same time that it improves the structure of the soil and encourages the growth of microbial soil life.

If you should apply alfalfa too thickly, it will swell with the moisture from rain or irrigation and will encourage rot if it is in contact with rhizomes. Fertilize in early spring (March), before bloom (July), and then again in September. In addition to alfalfa, Kremer uses fertilizers that are formulated as 10-10-10 or 12-12-12, whichever is cheaper, applying a 50-pound bag to an area about 100 by 100 feet.

Since these irises grow and reproduce at high rates, they should be divided more often than once-bloomers, as often as every two years or even every year for the most vigorous. In the garden, you might minimize the effect of this by having two clumps of each remontant iris and dividing half one year and half the next year. Kremer reports that 'English Cottage' is a reblooming iris that crowds itself so much that it will not bloom in the third year unless it's separated.

During the growing season, do not break off the flower stalks of remontant irises all the way to their sockets after blooming as you can with onetime spring bloomers. Cut the stalks with a sharp knife or garden scissors an inch or two above their bases so as not to remove buds of new flower stalks. In the fall, after rebloom, it is important to remove all bloom stalks to prevent rot.

What if an iris that is supposed to be remontant does not repeat its blooming period? Is something wrong with the iris or its location or the care you are giving it? If you have ordered your remontant irises from a location that is very different from yours, it might well be the environment that is lacking. It is quite likely, for instance, that irises from California will not perform in the same way in New England.

You increase your chances of success with reblooming irises if you get them from your own area—that way, you know that they will rebloom in similar situations. Although most irisarians say that a new remontant iris should bloom the first spring after planting and rebloom that same year, others suggest that you should be patient and give the iris a full year to adjust to your specific location.

The reblooming tall bearded iris 'Buckwheat', shown here in late October in St. Louis. (Photograph by Barbara Perry Lawton.)

71

ARIL AND ARILBRED IRISES

This group includes some of the most exotic-looking irises of the entire genus. The original species plus their hybrids plus the crosses between the arils and the more usual bearded (eupogon or pogon) irises result in flowers that are close to unbelievable. Rich colors, unusual patterns and exotic shapes are common in this lesser-known group of irises.

The somewhat-bearded iris group known as aril and arilbred irises includes the sections of the subgenus *Iris* of the *Iris* genus, known as *Oncocyclus*, *Regelia, Hexapogon* and *Pseudoregelia,* plus hybrids of these and also hybrids of these and some of the other bearded irises. Of these four subgenera, gardeners should be most concerned with learning about the first two sections, the *Oncocyclus* and *Regelia* irises, since the others are currently rare in the gardening world and not likely to be much better known over the next few years.

Two species of *Pseudoregelia* irises, *Iris kamaonensis* and *I. tigridia,* both dwarf mountain plants of eastern Asia, are sometimes seen in the gardens of iris specialists. These aril irises are very different from the other bearded irises and so are often not included under the bearded iris umbrella, even though they will hybridize with the more common bearded irises.

The arils are named for the white collar that surrounds the hilium (the spot that marks the attachment of the seed to the seedpod) of the seeds of these arils and arilbred irises. The white collar or aril on the seed is a fleshy appendage not found on the seeds of pogon irises. This aril may be as large as the rest of the seed. The aril of the *Oncocyclus* irises is especially large. The aril of the *Regelia* section irises also is fairly large, but the arils of the other irises in this grouping are small compared to the rest of the seed.

'Genetic Artist', a Regelia type of aril iris, captured in
Omaha, Nebraska. (Photograph by Jim Morris.)

HISTORY

Some people have speculated that the "lilies of the field" mentioned in the Bible were aril irises. The first verifiable record of arils dates to 1573 when an aril iris species, *Iris susiana,* was brought to Europe from Constantinople. Certainly this is possible since *Oncocyclus* irises are native to the Middle East, having been found from Israel, Jordan and Syria through Turkey, Iran and Iraq all the way to the Caucasus Mountains in southern Russia.

The "oncos" from the arid hot lands east of the Mediterranean Sea are desert plants that thrive on extreme heat with very little water. Those that are native to the mountains and high steppes are able to endure cold weather and more rainfall. There is also a lot of variation among the fifty-plus onco species that have been discovered and among the clones of individual species. Oncos are similar to each other in that they are rhizomatous and have stems with only one flower. They have conspicuous arils that are often pale or white. Most of them have broad diffuse beards and clearly defined signal patches at the ends of the beards that are darker than the ground color.

The eight known species of *Regelia* irises, although very similar to the *Oncocyclus* irises, usually have two flowers per stem and beards on both standards and falls. Their native territory picks up in northeastern Iran where the *Oncocyclus* irises peter out. Their comparatively small native area continues through the nearby central Asian portion of Russia. These irises naturally grow on rocky or sandy hills and have a dormant summer period.

Hybridization between the oncos and *Regelias* began in the late 1800s, resulting in many plants that were loaded with hybrid vigor and also were easy to cultivate. Some of these proved infertile and slowed breeding work in this century. The development of fully fertile tetraploids, those with twice the usual number of chromosomes, got off the ground after World War II.

In the 1950s, there was increased interest in growing both arils and arilbreds, and a study group organized the Southern California Iris Society in 1954 to that purpose. This fledgling group almost immediately became the Aril Society International (ASI), although all of the founders lived within 50 miles of Los Angeles. The group since has become a cooperating society of the American Iris Society. The first ASI yearbook was published in 1958 and included ten of the most eminent irisarians of Europe.

Breeding advances of arils and arilbreds have continued with the development of fully fertile, 44-chromosome (double the usual number of chromosomes, also expressed as 4n) tetraploids. Breeders are intercrossing and linebreeding new, fully fertile half-breds, and the number of introductions has risen. There now are aril and arilbred cultivars to grow in almost any climate. The Aril Society yearbooks continue to carry extensive information on hybridizing these unusual irises.

CHARACTERISTICS

The arillate irises have beards, although the beards of aril and arilbred irises are sparse, looking long and scraggly on the *Regelias* and like a wide fuzzy patch on the *Oncocycluses*. And they often are crossed with tall bearded, median and miniature dwarf bearded irises. That is my justification for including them at the end of the bearded iris section. Most books put the arils in a separate section, yet they are genetically close enough to cross with the eupogon, true-bearded irises.

The irises that fall within the horticultural classes of aril and arilbred irises are so very different from each other and so variable that one must have some understanding of the entire collective group in order to grasp the particulars. The name "aril," as we've already explained, refers to all irises and hybrids with arillate seeds, seeds with little fleshy white collars called arils. That characteristic is a botanical one. The term "arilbred" refers to hybrids that result from crosses of aril species plus hybrids of the aril species with true bearded (eupogon) irises.

Characteristics of the some fifty species of *Oncocyclus* irises, commonly called oncos, include overlapping standards that have a round, domed look. They may be tailored, ruffled or reflexed outward on the sides, a characteristic that is called flagging. The falls are also rounded and they usually tuck under the flower. The falls may be flaring, recurved, rolled under, concave or some combination of these traits. Standards are usually larger than the falls.

Stem heights range from a minute 3 inches to a tall 28 inches and but a single flower grows on each stem. Proportion usually is good, although there are exceptions with large flowers overwhelming short stems or small flowers stuck on tall stems. The stems are almost straight, may have leafy stem spathes and may be either thick and fleshy or thin and wiry.

Veining and stippling or dotting, in strong or muted shades, are an aril characteristic of the flowers' falls and may also occur on the standards. One of the most distinguishing features of onco flowers is the dark, round spot or "signal" that appears at the tip end of the wide beard. The beards are usually broad but may also be linear and range in color from white to nearly black. The flower colors range through a wide variety of colors, patterns and textures, including self, blend, bitone, bicolor and amoena.

Regelia irises of the aril class mostly have stems with two flowers each. Typically, these flowers have standards and falls that are much narrower than the oncos. Standards are sometimes referred to as pagoda-shaped. Both standards and falls are heavily veined. The beards are narrow and brightly colored, occurring on the falls and, to a lesser degree, on the standards. (Oncos, you remember, have beards only on the falls.) When there is a signal or spot at the end of the beard on each fall, it is usually small and occurs as a **V**-shaped color spot. The flowers have a more delicate appearance than the oncos and are small to medium in size. Each flower stem is slender and usually tall in proportion to the blossom size.

Hybrids made between *Regelia* and onco irises usually will have two buds per stem and a flower form that generally demonstrates more *Regelia* influence and traits than onco traits—that is, they will have heavy veining, a **V**-shaped signal and color spot. Lilac or lilac-rose ground colors will show dark violet or gray-purple veining with a dark signal spot. Both plants and flowers will be medium in size.

Section VIII, which discusses the botany of irises, offers the contemporary classification chart of the genus *Iris*. For the purposes of this chapter, it is probably enough to know that the subgenus *Iris* includes the pogon or bearded irises plus irises in the botanical sections *Psammiris* (closely related to the *Regelia* group), *Oncocyclus, Regelia, Hexapogon* and *Pseudoregelia*. Indeed, this may be more than you want to know.

CULTURE

Although arils and arilbreds may be difficult to grow in most parts of the United States where there are moist summers, they can easily be grown in warm, dry regions of our country, especially in places like the desert areas of Arizona and New Mexico. Increasingly, though, there are arils or arilbreds for just about every climate zone of the United States. The trick is to learn which ones will do well in your particular area. For that, you may have to contact local irisarians or commercial growers who specialize in irises.

One good piece of advice is to start with award winners that have had to prove themselves under a wide variety of conditions and climates. Aril and arilbred iris experts promise that if you can grow tall bearded irises successfully, you should be able to grow the fantastic arilbreds. First of all, select an area with plenty of sun and good drainage, a soil that would suit tall bearded irises or median bearded irises. Gardens with very heavy soils or enough rain to promote rot in tall bearded irises will present a problem for arilbreds as well.

Good sharp drainage will be the key to success. Raised beds may be the answer for those with heavy soil, poor drainage or too much annual rainfall. Arilbreds can tolerate several times the average rainfall of arils' native lands if, and only if, the drainage is excellent. Raised beds and specially prepared soil may be the best answer for some regions.

Prepare the iris bed several weeks ahead of time, mixing in fertilizer and water, then allowing the soil to settle. When ready to plant, make two holes separated by a narrow ridge and press a rhizome into the ridge. Spread the roots to both sides and down. Fill the hole with soil, making sure there are no air pockets around the rhizome and its roots. The top of the rhizome should be about 1 to 2 inches below ground level in heavy soil, 2 to 3 inches below ground level in sandy soil. Place plants about a foot apart.

Keep the root zone moist but not soggy throughout the growing season. Regularly check the soil for moisture to a depth of 3 to 4 inches. Apply a general-purpose fertilizer in the fall and in early spring. Arilbreds are notoriously heavy feeders, so be loyal to your fertilizer program. Have your soil tested to see what is lacking—that is the only sure way to intelligently decide on a fertilizer program. If your soils are acid or neutral, raise the pH level with additions of dolomitic limestone, which will encourage growth and cut down on rot. Once the irises have bloomed, required care will depend on your climate. If summers tend to be dry in your region, stop watering and leave the plants in the ground. Arils and arilbred irises prefer soil with a higher pH than other bearded irises.

Note that the arilbreds, combinations of arils and the bearded irises, are far easier to grow than the original *Oncocyclus* iris species from the Near East that grow during cooler, wetter winters and go dormant during hot dry summers. If you live in the desert Southwest, you may be able to grow the original aril species, as the climate would be similar to that of their native

'Bronie Comet', a popular arilbred iris, shown here at the Missouri Botanical Garden. (Photograph by Barbara Perry Lawton.)

77

The arilbred iris 'Cool Oasis', shown here in an Arizona garden.
(Photograph by Jim Morris.)

lands. In other parts of the country, some people treat the original aril species as annuals and are pleased with their performance, although not everyone has been able to do that successfully.

In the desert Southwest, some shade in the afternoon would be appreciated. The same is true for areas at high altitude that also have strong sun all day that can burn both plants and people. Note that you will have to protect onco irises from excessive summer moisture—some use overhead awnings or canopies. *Regelias,* on the other hand, are somewhat more tolerant of moist conditions.

Growers with wet summer climates usually are the ones who have problems growing arils and arilbred irises. England, where many of the early experiments in growing this interesting group of irises took place, is a notoriously poor place for growing arils. Therefore, you don't hear many recommendations from the English. On the other hand, our desert Southwest is a good match for the arils' original climate. And, in other parts of our country as well, gardeners may be able to just plant the arils and arilbreds in with their tall bearded irises and they may do quite well.

The flip side of growing arils and arilbreds in some parts of the desert Southwest is that the winds may blow so much sand that they cover the iris plants too deep for blooming. They then have to be disinterred and cleaned off when growth starts. At the same time, the sand mounds provide good insulation for iris clumps in the summer when the heat averages over 100 degrees F and humidity may be high after a rain.

Growing arils and arilbred irises in the interior of the United States, in places like Kentucky, will take some extra effort because of the wide variation of the weather from year to year and within each year. Regions like the upper Mississippi and Ohio Valleys display a continental climate at its best and worst. Cold, dry Canadian air constantly wars with warm, moist Gulf air. Trial and error will come into play for gardeners in this erratic climate. The keys, of course, will be to avoid drainage problems and the effects of excessive water during spring and summer rains. Advice from area iris experts will be of more importance when growing arils and arilbreds than with most other irises.

The best time for planting arilbred irises is during the period when they are coming out of dormancy. Planting during summer heat is stressful, and so is planting during the late fall prior to severe winter weather. The exact time for optimum planting will depend on the climate. Gardeners in northern

The arilbred iris 'Engraved', in the Smith Garden, Kirkwood, Missouri. (Photograph by Riley Probst.)

states sometimes grow aril irises in pots that they plunge into the garden soil in October, then lift out and store in midsummer. Other experts recommend never growing arils in pots because their rhizomes and roots need to spread out. Still others lift aril irises out of the ground in July and store them in vermiculite or sand until October, when they put them back into the ground. These practices are, I suspect, to avoid the ravages of rainy summer weather.

Where they can be left in the ground during the summer, plant them after the worst of the summer heat when they are starting to break summer dormancy. If you have new rhizomes, plant them at the same time, when arils already in the ground are breaking dormancy. There seem to be as many or more theories on growing aril irises than there are different growing environments in this large country of ours.

In dividing these irises, note that many of the arils and arilbreds increase rapidly and will have to be divided every year or two to avoid overcrowding. Follow the same schedule of digging and planting soon after the worst of the summer heat when there is still time for root growth before the hard cold of winter.

Clearly, one thing is for sure. The book is still being written on arils and arilbreds. It will be interesting to see what the next few decades will bring, both in new cultivars and ease of cultivation.

The Beardless Irises

The Siberian iris 'Chilled Wine', in a Pennsylvania garden. (Photograph by Jim Morris.)

SIBERIAN IRISES

The beauty and grace of Siberian irises add a special dimension to any garden bed or border. When they are in bloom, the delicate-looking flowers float like butterflies above the slim swordlike leaves. When they are not in bloom, the foliage adds a handsome linear quality to the texture of the garden.

Siberian irises are one of the best known and best loved of the beardless irises. The slender leaves of Siberian irises are a design asset in themselves, but when topped by branched stalks, each bearing up to nine or more flowers, the effect is sensational. If I had to choose only one iris type, the Siberian irises might well be that one. Fortunately, most of us can admire and easily grow a number of different kinds of irises.

HISTORY

Iris sibirica and *I. sanguinea*, the two species that botanists accept as major species of the Siberian series of beardless irises, undoubtedly have been cultivated for over two centuries. *I. sibirica*, a plant of wet meadows from central Europe and northern Italy all the way to the land west of Lake Baikal in Russia, is a handsome iris that undoubtedly appeared in early gardens. The violet-blue to blue flowers usually have darker veins and have been bred into cultivars that range from purest white to deep violet blue.

I. sibirica was first recorded and named by Linnaeus in 1754. Today, a number of species are included within the series *Sibiricae*, of the section *Limniris*, which is part of the beardless iris subgenus *Limniris*. (For more on the botany of irises, see section VIII.) *I. sanguinea*, originally named *I. orientalis*, was next

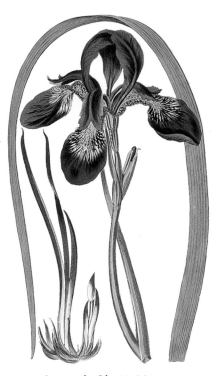

Iris siberica, *the Siberian iris, originally native to central and eastern Europe and east to Japan.*

83

The Siberian iris 'Silver Illusion', in a Missouri garden. (Photograph by Jim Morris.)

discovered and described by Thunberg in 1794. This iris originally grew from the land east of Lake Baikal all the way to Japan. The majority of our Siberian iris cultivars derive from these two species, *I. sibirica* and *I. sanguinea*.

In addition to these two species, botanists recognize eight other species in the series *Sibiricae*, all from central and eastern Asia. These were discovered and named between 1875 and 1933. The plants of all ten species of this series are quite tall and thrive in the damp soil of mountain meadows and thin woodlands. Taxonomist Brian Mathew does not divide these ten species into yet another botanical subgroup as many have in the past. He says in *The Iris* that further splitting of the beardless irises is hard to justify morphologically. I'm sure you agree.

The beauty of the plants and their blooms and the ease of growing the Siberian irises combined to make them irresistible to plant breeders. By the 1920s and 1930s, breeders in Canada and the United States were making great strides in selecting improved natural crosses of these handsome plants. They were selecting and naming superior plants from parent plants that had been bee-pollinated.

According to Siberian iris breeder Anna Mae Miller of Kalamazoo, Michigan, the real progress in garden varieties of Siberian irises began after the 1960s when crosses were controlled and particular qualities could be contributed by selecting parents that passed certain attributes on to the offspring. Among the special qualities that Siberian iris breeders consider are branching of flower stalks, plant vigor and foliage quality. In Siberian iris flowers, breeders look for ruffling, improved and new colors and good proportion.

CHARACTERISTICS

The foliage of Siberian irises ranges from rich green to glaucous blue-green with leaves that are narrow and erect. The foliage rises above slender rhizomes. Each tall clump makes a statement in the garden landscape, providing a focal point that enhances the bed or border. While flower size and the height of the flower stalks should be in proportion to each other, the tall stalks of Siberian irises may carry small flowers gracefully on slender stalks that sway over the foliage.

Well-branched stalks are an asset so long as the stalks and flowers are well spaced and don't interfere with one another. Typically, there will be a stalk plus two major branches so that flowers are borne on three different levels. Bracts should be in proportion to the stalks, neither too wide nor too long, and should remain colored and healthy after the blooming season is past. Breeders and growers alike give high points to a long sequence of bud bloom, as that can appreciably lengthen the blooming season.

The graceful flowers must be in proportion to the plant. Ruffled flowers are often pleasing in contrast to the more normal yet handsome tailored types. The falls of Siberian irises influence the beauty of the flowers, varying from narrow to round and from vertical to horizontal. Although narrow strappy falls are undesirable, those with rounded or oval shapes that arch downward are as desirable as the more flaring types.

The flower standards vary widely in size, shape and position, with some being inconspicuous while others are relatively large and even arched or domed. The overall effect and grace of the flower are what counts. The falls may have unusual texture—silky, shiny, rough, metallic or velvety. Texture is a surface quality primarily of the falls that influences the impact of color by reflecting or absorbing light. Siberian iris flowers should remain fresh for several days.

Look for varieties known for their long-lasting flowers. Ample substance, strength and firmness of the flowers are important to their lasting quality. Anna Mae Miller points out that there are Siberian cultivars that bloom for up to eighteen days. "It takes just as much weeding time, fertilizer and TLC for inferior plants as for superior ones!" she says.

Colors range from nearly black and wine reds to purples, lavenders and blues, to pinks, whites and yellows. The colors of the flowers should be clean and clear and should not change significantly until aging of the flowers is advanced.

CULTURE

Most gardeners find these irises both reliable and easy to grow. In general, the beardless irises require more water and an acid soil. This is in contrast to the general cultural requirements for bearded irises that thrive with less water and in a more nearly neutral soil. They are easy to grow just about anywhere, although they will bloom less, if at all, in shady sites.

New roots begin to grow shortly after blooming and that seems to be a good time to divide Siberian irises. Therefore, you can successfully divide and plant these irises after the blooming season in July or August when they will have ample time to grow new roots and re-anchor themselves to the soil before cold weather.

The Siberian iris 'Dutch', named for President Reagan, shown in a Washington State garden. (Photograph by Jim Morris.)

Many gardeners have success with planting Siberians in the early fall. In the early spring, when the plants are under 3 to 4 inches tall, is another time when it is easy to divide and move Siberian irises. Whatever timing you choose, be sure they have time for the rhizomes to begin growing new roots before the rigors of winter or summer. Plant the rhizomes horizontally with the foliage side up so that the tops of the rhizomes are 2 to 3 inches below the soil surface.

Once established, they will readily naturalize in the landscape, providing blooms year after year as reliably as naturalized daffodils. The single qualification is that they have an acid soil and, for most of the garden cultivars, ample moisture, although once they are established, they can tolerate droughty periods fairly well. Though even moisture is needed, good drainage is also appreciated. Plan to incorporate plenty of humus, sphagnum peat moss, compost, well-rotted manure or other organic material into the soil. Although many growers recommend keeping the soil at a pH of about 5.8, others report that the pH is not all that important. One thing is for sure, plants grown in a highly organic soil are more tolerant of a wide range of environmental factors, including pH, than are plants grown in a more mineral soil.

While highly organic soil and consistent moisture head the catechism for growers of Siberian irises, there always will be those exceptions that may well thrive in or at least tolerate alkalinity and a heavy clay soil. A valuable thing to remember when gardening is that you should never say "never," and also should never say "always."

When Siberian iris clumps outgrow their allotted space or when you want to divide them in order to spread them around, choose a cool, invigorating day to work. The roots are fibrous and thick, growing from slender rhizomes. Thus they may be hard to split, calling for a knife or sharp spade. When making divisions for replanting, be sure that each division has about a half dozen or more fans of foliage and protect the roots from drying out during the replanting process. Make the new planting holes large enough to spread the roots, then tamp the soil gently into the hole and water the newly planted irises thoroughly.

Anna Mae Miller recommends soaking Siberian iris divisions overnight, especially if they are plants that have been shipped to you. The roots must never dry out. Water the planting hole, plant the iris divisions, firm soil over the roots and then water well to get rid of air pockets. Apparently, air pockets in the soil are the real bugaboo of Siberians, especially when you are planting bare-rooted specimens. Once you have set the roots in the planting hole, add soil little by little and tamp each addition down to eliminate those pesky air pockets. Keep well watered until foliage begins to grow. Although some varieties of Siberian irises can stand periods of drought, they are not as tolerant of very dry conditions as the tall bearded irises.

Iris hartwegii growing in the wild in California's Sierra Nevada mountains. (Photograph by Jim Morris.)

PACIFIC COAST IRISES

Pacific Coast irises (PC) comprise a group of some eleven species that are native primarily to lightly wooded mountainous areas from California north along the coasts of Oregon and Washington. Most are native to the coastal ranges of California, Oregon and Washington. Four of these species also occur on the western slopes of the Cascade Mountains of Oregon and the Sierra Nevada of California. Two, *Iris Hartwegii* and *I. munzii,* are endemic to the Sierra Nevada, and one, *I. Hartwegii* subspecies *australis,* is native to the San Bernardino Mountains of southern California.

Iris douglasiana, *best known species of Pacific Coast irises.*

The Pacific Coast native species *Iris douglasiana* grows on the bluffs overlooking the Pacific Ocean and on the gritty windblown land just inland from the ocean beaches. This species also grows in heavy soil on disturbed land where lumbering and fires have taken their toll in deforestation. The other ten species of the Pacific Coast iris group grow well in semishady spots with neutral to slightly acid soil that drains well and is somewhat gritty.

The beardless irises of the series *Californicae,* like their cousins the Siberian, Louisiana and Japanese irises, fall within the section *Limniris* of the *Iris* subgenus *Limniris.* The Pacific Coast irises, usually quite dwarf in size, freely cross in the wild and are easily hybridized. The PC irises also will cross with the 40-chromosome Siberian irises to produce usually sterile cultivars called "Cal-Sibes."

The natives bloom in a multitude of hues from cream and yellow through pinks, orange-pinks, to pale blue or lavender and even deep purple. The flowers are about the size of those of Siberian irises but more compact and often with horizontal falls that may be either narrow and pointed or round and wide. Many of the modern PC cultivars are ruffled and have a luminous quality that is breathtaking. A slight wash of turquoise that lights up the entire flower is common in cultivars with *I. munzii* in their background, but almost nonexistent in others.

HISTORY

Compared to most other irises, the Pacific Coast irises have a short history because they weren't discovered and brought into cultivation until California was settled by the European pioneers and miners, primarily in the nineteenth century. Their botanical classification and relationships were defined in the late 1950s by Lee W. Lenz, Ph.D., of the Rancho Santa Ana Botanic Garden in Claremont, California. It was he who defined the eleven species and five subspecies that taxonomist Brian Mathew and other botanists accept today.

These irises probably are originally from Asia and crossed over to North America via the isthmus that spanned the Bering Sea in ancient times. From the region of the Bering Strait, the plants slowly made their way down to the West Coast of the United States. The Cascade and Sierra Nevada ranges prevented eastward migration of the Pacific Coast native irises.

Masses of native irises in mountain meadows must have astounded those early travelers as they made their way across the mountains to seek their fortunes in California, Oregon and Washington. Lewis and Adele Lawyer, breeders of Pacific Coast native irises, note that masses of native irises in mountain meadows were compared to a blue lake in the writings of pioneers. This PC is a meadow and bog iris that can make thick clumps up to several acres in size.

The Lawyers report that *Iris douglasiana* also tends to grow in large patches near and often in sight of the ocean, as in Marin County, California. *I. tenax* makes individual clumps, but the Lawyers have never seen it coalesced into thick masses. It is ironic, the Lawyers observe, that PCs tend to flourish following a clear-cut of forest trees. They come out as if by spontaneous generation, flourish for a few years, then gradually fade away as the trees grow back. Then they apparently remain there unnoticed until another forest catastrophe occurs. Today, it is more and more difficult to find patches of PCs growing wild. Many of their favorite habitats have disappeared, victims of California's booming population and massive housing developments.

The Pacific Coast native, Iris tenax, in the Silverberg Garden in Oregon. (Photograph by Jim Morris.)

Iris tenax was among the first of the Pacific Coast irises to be introduced to England. David Douglas collected seeds of this species on the lower Columbia River, probably near Fort Vancouver, and it was named and illustrated in the botanical *Registry* of 1829. William Rickatson Dykes, author of *The Genus Iris* and the expert for whom the Dykes Medal is named, and Amos Perry, another famous English hybridizer, were making crosses of Pacific Coast irises around the turn of the century. Dykes was an English schoolmaster in Godalming. Perry, of Enfield, England, had abandoned irises but then took them up again.

Iris innominata, a small, graceful Pacific Coast iris, became a cornerstone of breeding programs because it gave its best qualities to hybrids and crosses, fostering vigor, glossy foliage and an array of new flower colors. This species occurs in pure stands of both yellow and purple. It was discovered in 1928 by Mrs. John R. Leach, a well-known Portland botanist, gardener and explorer.

During the same period, Dr. Mathew Riddle collected a pound or so of *I. innominata* seed while on fishing trips in southwestern Oregon. He tucked the seeds into his lunch bag and grew them in his own garden. He also sent a jarful of *innominata* seeds to Professor Sydney B. Mitchell of Berkeley, California.

Since Mitchell was the American Iris Society chairman for species irises, he distributed a quantity of *I. innominata* seed to growers and breeders

Iris tenax, *a graceful Pacific Coast species iris native to the northwestern United States.*

91

The Pacific Coast iris 'Big Wheel' in a San Jose, California garden. (Photograph by Jim Morris.)

around the world. Soon this iris was lending itself to breeding programs in many places far from California. Mitchell also grew and promoted *I. douglasiana,* another fine PC iris species that was used along with *I. innominata* to make elegant crosses, resulting in many promising new cultivars. Mitchell specialized in bee crosses, systematically roguing out lesser plants so that the bees could choose from among the best Pacific Coast irises.

Margaret Brummit of England led the way in the breeding of *I. innominata* and *I. douglasiana. I. douglasiana* was largely the cornerstone of the southern California breeding programs. The southern California breeders of PCs were dominant in the early U.S. breeding scene. PC breeders Lewis and Adele Lawyer observe that it's a pity that *I. tenax,* a species that could certainly contribute to freeze resistance, has been so little used in the hundreds of PC cultivars. This is primarily because it does not perform well in California, where the bulk of the breeding has been done.

George Stambach was another early breeder of Pacific Coast native irises. Even in his later years during the 1960s, he continued to hybridize and grow these irises. The Society for Pacific Coast Native Irises was a dream of his that became a reality in the 1970s, during his lifetime. The society, a section of AIS, was conceived and organized one day after a meeting of the Southern California Iris Society. Stambach's enthusiasm was catching. He gave away PC iris seeds at every iris meeting and mailed seed all over the world.

Specialists in Pacific Coast irises as well as other wildflowers are quick to point out that research on native irises and other plants, plus public support for that research, is tougher and tougher to find. The range of wild irises is diminishing rapidly and thus it is important for admirers of these eleven species to gather enough information about their biology before it is too late.

The Pacific Coast native irises were grown mostly in England, Australia and New Zealand until the late 1960s, when irisarians in the United States rediscovered them. Interestingly, in the 1920s there were only two PC breeders, Dykes and Perry, both from England. By the 1940s, there were six U.S. PC hybridizers and one from England, and in the 1960s, there were ten from the United States and three from England. Serious hybridizing of PCs continues today, primarily in the States and in England.

The latest trend in this realm is crosses between PC irises and the 40-chromosome Siberian irises, resulting in Cal-Sibes, which promise to open a whole new world of beauty for gardeners and growers alike. The usually sterile Cal-Sibes are plants for neutral to slightly acid soils and full sun to partial shade. They need less summer soil moisture than their Siberian iris parents and also can tolerate more water than their Pacific Coast iris parents. It looks as though these cross-species irises will have a wider range of environmental tolerance than the straight PC irises, and so promise to thrive in many more regions.

The members of the Society for Pacific Coast Native Irises, a section of the American Iris Society, have established a tradition of annual expeditions to visit and study wild populations of these irises. They report their activities in their *Almanac: Society for Pacific Coast Native Irises,* which began publication in 1972.

CHARACTERISTICS

The eleven species that make up the Californian class of irises are singular in that they all are native to the Pacific Coast states of California, Oregon and Washington. Their chromosome count (2n), the number you would find in any of the species, is 40—or 20 pairs of chromosomes. These irises generally are quite dwarf with unbranched flower stems, slender grassy leaves, tough rhizomes and wiry roots.

Exceptions to this are *Iris douglasiana* and especially *I. munzii,* which can produce flower stalks as tall as 3 feet. These two species also have longer, broader leaves. *I. munzii* doesn't branch but can produce four flowers per spathe. *I. douglasiana* branches and can produce three flowers per spathe. Crosses between these two species can produce branched flower stems with up to four flowers per spathe, a total of eight to eighteen flowers per stalk. The Lawyers have observed single flower stalks with up to three flowers open at one time. With the exception of *I. tenax* and *I. hartwegii*, which are deciduous, the PC native irises are evergreen.

    I. douglasiana and *I. innominata* are the two species that serve as the backbone of contemporary PC hybrids. *I. douglasiana*, with the widest distribution of all the PC irises, grows easily and quickly from seed and has flowers of many colors, from white through azure through lavender and purple. *I. innominata* is particularly noted for its deep yellow and golden flowers. Both are worthy additions to gardens. *I. innominata*, native to Oregon, thrives under cool growing conditions and will not do well in other climates. Its grass-like foliage gives the plants a finely delicate look.

    A few years ago, Lewis and Adele Lawyer surveyed named cultivars to see what species were directly involved in their background. One hundred and twenty-eight had *douglasiana* in their immediate background, while eighty-nine traced to *innominata*, twenty-nine to *tenax* and twenty to *munzii*. Since then, it is likely that *I. munzii* has surpassed *I. tenax*.

    The most cold-hardy of the PC irises is *I. tenax*, a native to the western side of the Cascade Mountains. It is also used in hybridizing programs. This iris, a deciduous species, grows into attractive clumps with many flowers. While these three species have played the major roles in modern PC hybrids, the other species have been a part of some hybridizing programs, playing a much lesser part in the background of garden cultivars.

    Plants of this class of irises grow in mountainous and open forested regions, with the exception that *I. douglasiana* grows near the ocean on windy bluffs and bare land that has recently been cleared. This is a widely grown Pacific Coast native iris, an excellent garden plant undoubtedly because of its wide range of adaptability. It also is geographically the most widespread of these irises. *I. douglasiana* will grow in well-draining gritty soils amended with compost or in heavy clay soils and is extremely vigorous. This species has leaves up to 1/8 inch in width and 12 to 40 inches in length. Flower colors range from cream to lavender to red-purple with occasional blue and albino forms. The plants form large circular mats of vigorous growth.

Pacific Coast iris seedlings pictured in the Jones Garden of Portland, Oregon. (Photograph by Jim Morris.)

PC flowers are irislike in character, with falls that flare rather than droop or curve down. The different species are quite variable, especially in their colors. In gardens, the species crossbreed easily, often producing handsome offspring.

CULTURE

Although most of those growing Pacific Coast irises in the United States live in roughly the same territories as the native Californian irises, increasing numbers of home gardeners and irisarians are successfully growing these beautiful species and cultivars in other regions of the country, including Arizona, Maine, Arkansas and Nebraska. If they can all grow these irises in their diverse regions, you may be able to have some success in your state.

This class of irises is well suited for gardens in its native lands. It is hard to find similar climates in the United States, climates like the West Coast where you can find places with close to six months without rain. You would be wise to check with iris fanciers in your neighborhood before launching a program of growing that may demand more effort than it's worth—in other words, Pacific Coast native irises will not thrive in all locations. Gardeners in England, New Zealand and Canada are among those in other countries who are trying their luck with these irises.

Gritty well-draining soil with plenty of organic matter and a pH that is within the range of slightly acid to neutral is what will suit Pacific Coast irises very well. It is likely that they will not do well where the soil has a pH that is above 7.0. Protection from hot afternoon sun will be beneficial. A site that is on a moist slope or along a stream in a region where summers are long and dry will encourage these irises to thrive.

The best environment for these irises is one with cool, moist winters and long, dry, warm summers. The combination of hot sun and rain will encourage crown rot—plants in this type of climate are usually lost. Their growing cycle is such that they begin to grow when rainy fall weather arrives and reach their peak of growth in spring and early summer. After they bloom and set seed, they begin a dormant period during the dry summer season of their native lands.

Those who grow these irises in eastern and midwestern states should protect the roots from freezing with winter mulches and see that they have good air circulation in the summer to protect from fungal diseases. Gardeners outside of PCs' natural habitats will find that growing them from seed is generally more successful than growing from rhizomes or transplants.

Pacific Coast native irises are best transplanted before the plants reach their blooming period and well before they begin their summer dormant period. Dividing and transplanting while they are in active growth means that they have a good root system that will help them stand the shock of transplanting.

The Lawyers, with years of experience in growing Pacific Coast irises, are confident that PCs eventually will adapt to somewhat similar climates. They already have adapted to many diverse microclimates on the West Coast. Their natural habitats, from Washington all the way down to California, and from the seacoast to the 7,000-foot Sierra Nevadas, are extremely diverse. Where the Lawyers live in Oakland, California, the PCs thrive with so little care that landscape gardeners use them by the thousands. At peak bloom, the Lawyers' garden has 2,000 open blooms.

LOUISIANA IRISES

The Cajuns of Louisiana called these irises snake flowers when they saw them growing in the swamps. Strangely, the flowers even smell like snakes. These beauties are native Americans. Louisiana iris species grow in the southern United States in bogs, marshes and swamps along the Gulf Coast from the Florida panhandle to Texas, and along the Mississippi River Valley as far north as the mouth of the Ohio River.

Botanically (see also section VIII), they are in the *Limniris* subgenus of the genus *Iris*. Further, they are in the *Limniris* section of the *Limniris* subgenus, the section that includes all of the irises classed as beardless. My favorite beardless garden irises are classed within the *Limniris* section—Siberian, Japanese and Louisiana irises, to name a few.

The Louisiana irises, which are in the *Hexagonae* series of the *Limniris* section, are admired for their large flowers and robust growth. Botanists disagree on the classification of the Louisiana irises, some preferring to say that there are ten species in this group, while others are equally in favor of as few as three species in this iris class. In the world of botany, it seems to depend on whether you are a "lumper" who prefers to keep plants in larger taxonomic classes or a "splitter" who prefers to break out every variation of plant form into a different species. Botanist Brian Mathew, an expert on iris classification, names *Iris hexagona* as the type species.

The brilliant colors of these irises, often seen in the wild in masses for miles along the bayous of Louisiana, range from bronze and copper through pink, rose, red and yellow to blue and violet. These have been extensively

Iris hexagona, *a Louisiana iris, one of the seven Louisiana iris species.*

97

hybridized, both naturally and by humans. These water irises all have large seeds that disperse by floating here and there. The light corky outer coating of the seeds enables them to float.

HISTORY

"It is a magnificent Iris with broad foliage and stems over 3 feet high," said Thomas Walter in first describing *Iris hexagona* in his *Flora caroliniana* in 1788. This Louisiana iris is native to the southeastern United States, an area that is farther east than the other species of Louisianas. The large flowers are lavender to blue-purple with yellow signal areas along the middle of the falls. The *Botanical Magazine* named, described and illustrated the distinctive form, coloration and habit of *Iris fulva* in 1812. Though its flowers are smaller than those of other Louisianas, they are striking in shades of terra-cotta, orange-red, red and copper.

Mathew also includes *I. brevicaulis,* a shorter iris with bright violet-blue flowers; *I. giganticaerulea,* a very tall plant with pale to dark-blue or white flowers marked by yellow signal ridges on the falls; and *I. nelsonii,* the red-flowered irises long known as Abbeville Reds.

The New York Botanical Garden's Dr. John K. Small is the man who put Louisiana irises on the map. He saw fields of irises from a train while traveling through southern Louisiana in 1920 and was astounded by their beauty and vast numbers. In 1925, he called Louisiana the "iris center of the universe" and, over the next years, collected these irises extensively. In 1931 he, along with E. J. Alexander, described a number of species. His published articles describing Louisiana irises and introducing them to the American public even made *The New York Times.*

During the 1930s, species and natural hybrids of Louisiana irises were collected and grown in gardens. It was Small who collected and named one of the most spectacular of irises, *Iris giganticaerulea.* Flower colors of this giant, which grows up to 6 feet tall, range from blue to indigo with yellow signal ridges down the middle of the falls.

More recently, botanists including Brian Mathew have come to believe that many of the irises collected by Small did not represent the entire group of Louisiana irises in the *Hexagonae* series but rather a fairly small group of closely related irises plus their naturally occurring hybrids, most from within the species *I. nelsonii.* Small had described over seventy species of wild irises,

The Louisiana iris 'This I Love' from the Loden garden in Mississippi. (Photograph by Jim Morris.)

but it turned out that in his enthusiasm he often was describing natural hybrids among species. More about the botanical classification of these and other irises can be found in section VIII on the botany of irises. These irises came to be known as "Abbeville Irises" because they grew wild in the Abbeville swamp of Vermilion Parish in south-central Louisiana.

Southern gardeners, beginning to realize what treasures they had in their swamps and waterways, also began to collect and hybridize the Louisiana irises. By 1941, these irises had become so popular that growers and hybridizers established the Society for Louisiana Irises (SLI), a cooperating society of the American Iris Society. Today, we find Louisiana iris enthusiasts throughout the United States and, in addition, in Germany, Japan and Australia; but where summers are cool, the bloom isn't as heavy as in those places with hot humid summers.

Some experts have theorized that the seeds floated down the Mississippi River system from colder climes, which would account for the fact that they have proven hardy as far north as Canada when provided with winter protection from cold wind and freeze-thaw cycles. Could it be that Louisiana irises are refugees from the Wisconsin Ice Age, the last great ice age that occurred some 75,000 years ago and lasted until only 10,000 years ago?

Remnants of other plant and animal life that fled before the great stretches of ice fields can still be found in the Ozark Mountains and farther south. *Iris fulva* grows in wet, sunny to partly shady sites in swamps or by streams as far north as Missouri and Ohio. Louisiana iris hybridizer Melody Wilhoit of Kansas, Illinois, has found *I. fulva* growing in southern Illinois and southern Indiana. Its smallish coppery red to orange-red flowers occur in April to May. Variations with yellow or even albino white are known in this species.

The Louisiana iris 'E.C. Everingham' hybridized in Australia. (Photograph by Jim Morris.)

The Society for Louisiana Irises members are dedicated not just to the development and cultivation of garden varieties but also to the preservation of the native species in the wild. There also had been a separate organization with similar aims called the Louisiana Iris Society of America (LISA). In 1992 the AIS board of directors approved the merger of the two groups into the Society for Louisiana Irises. Members of LISA were given memberships in the new combined organization.

Until the 1950s, there were huge areas of giant blue (*I. giganticaerulea*) native irises in the swamps of southwestern Louisiana. When Hurricane Audrey pounded Louisiana in 1957, the saltwater driven by the winds killed most of the plants. In other areas where Louisiana irises are native, their numbers have been depleted by drainage projects and development. The expansion of New Orleans did away with some giant stands of wild irises.

CHARACTERISTICS

In judging Louisiana irises according to the standards described in the AIS judging manual, the flower stalk should be straight or gracefully curved, except in the case of varieties with *I. brevicaulis* in their background—those will have the zigzag characteristic of that species. The height of the stalk should be in proportion to the blooms.

Flower buds should be spaced so that there is no interference with the foliage, and there should be a minimum of six buds per flower stalk. As to flower form, any form is acceptable that is typical of that variety. The color should be fresh and clear. All of the primary colors and their combinations are found in the Louisiana species and their hybrids. Louisianas may have flowers of bright, pleasing, blended colors and bicolors with harmonic color contrasts. They may display new color patterns including pronounced veining, spray patterns or halos.

Louisiana irises have flowers of many types including forms that are flat, flaring, pendent, recurving, open, overlapping, cartwheel and double or semidouble. The standards and falls may be ruffled. The style arms, very important to the beauty of these irises, may be in a different color than the standards and falls or they may be ruffled or edged with a different color. Signals, markings that may appear in the same location where beards are found in bearded irises, are typically orange or yellow and vary from nearly absent to very large. Some Louisiana iris cultivars have signals on both standards and falls and some have line signals referred to as crests that are raised and pubescent. There is so much variety to Louisianas that one must know a great deal in order to judge what is the ideal for the varieties.

Marvelous plants for a bog or water garden, the Louisiana irises also are handsome choices for herbaceous beds and borders. They are beautiful as cut flowers and easy to arrange. When the flower stalks are cut, the buds continue to open and the flowers will last several days. The flower stalks range from 1 to 5 feet in height.

These are excellent choices for gardens in the southern states, especially along the Gulf Coast and in Florida where bearded irises do not thrive

The Louisiana iris 'Charlie's Felicia' in a Georgia garden. (Photograph by Jim Morris.)

in the hot humid climate. Although native to the bayous, swamps and bogs of our South, Louisiana irises are adaptable to garden culture throughout the United States. They will also thrive in other countries, especially those with climates similar to Louisiana's, including parts of South Africa. Some enthusiasts have even grown them in northern Germany although they will bloom only sparsely there because of the cool summers.

It has only been in the past half century that Louisianas have gained the attention of breeders and growers. Today's hybrids bloom in all colors and color combinations. From the native shades of violet, blue, red, orange, yellow and white have come all tints and shades. It is the Louisiana irises that have added red to the iris palette.

Not as widely known as the bearded irises every gardener grows, the Louisianas have many variations in flower form and size as well as color, making them fascinating choices for perennial gardens. The blooming period, which

101

follows that of the bearded irises, can last from six weeks to two months, an advantage not found in many perennials.

CULTURE

Many gardeners claim that Louisiana irises are the easiest to grow of all the beardless irises. Unless you plan to show them, they don't need very much care. If you do plan to show them, you may have to take measures to keep slugs and snails away from flower stems and foliage. They can leave unattractive chew marks.

Louisiana irises, like other beardless irises, require an acid soil in order to thrive. Make your soil more acid by adding 1 or 2 pounds of agricultural sulfur and plenty of humus or compost to each 100 square feet. Well-rotted manure, compost, sphagnum peat moss, rotted hay and straw are all good soil additives that will increase the organic content of the soil and also improve soil structure. Don't add so much that the soil structure is light because then Louisiana irises may topple over when wind and rain arrive. Mix it in thoroughly and let it settle for two to three weeks, then test the soil pH. Repeat the sulfur amendment if the pH is still too high.

Lowering soil pH is more difficult than raising it. The speed with which sulfur will lower the pH will be greater in warm, wet weather and in light soils. In the Midwest, the effect of sulfur treatments for soil with a high pH will last about three years, less if in water. Louisiana irises will clearly indicate when the soil is becoming too sweet—they will turn a sickly yellow. Note that the normal dormant color of the foliage is pale, almost white. Once the weather warms, they will quickly turn green once again.

Melody Wilhoit notes that some varieties of Louisiana irises have lighter green foliage naturally. Those varieties with *Iris brevicaulis* (syn. *I. foliosa*) in their background tend to have blue-green foliage. The blue-green foliage is more disease resistant, including more rust resistant.

Heavy clay soils will suit Louisiana irises just fine. The heavy soil holds moisture well and also will help keep the flower stalks erect. Plan to plant or transplant Louisianas in mid- to late August. They should not be moved in the summer heat. Once planted, the soil must be kept moist.

Mulch Louisiana irises throughout the year to keep them at their best, especially in more northern states where winters may be severe. During the winter, top the mulch with a fluffy layer of old hay or straw. Any good organic

102

matter will serve as mulch if you have no hay or straw—sphagnum peat moss, compost, shredded bark, pine needles, shredded leaves or bush trimmings.

These irises are heavy feeders and so will perform very well if you give them a generous feeding of well-rotted steer or chicken manure after planting and right after they bloom. If you prefer to use a manufactured fertilizer, use an acid type, the kind that is formulated for azaleas and rhododendrons, to feed Louisiana irises. Fertilize when the plants are beginning to green up and again when they finish blooming. During the hot season, fertilize them and keep them well watered. Don't let them go dormant or you may lose them.

Although you can grow these irises in regular garden beds, marsh or bog culture is easiest of all since these are plants of wet habitats in the wild. It is best if you can control the water level to match what happens in the wild. That way, you can lower the water in the fall to plant or redo the bed. Then the water should be at soil level during the winter months so that new growth receives ample exposure to the air. When the foliage has grown taller, you can raise the water level to somewhere between 4 and 8 inches according to members of the Society for Louisiana Irises. While Louisiana irises require plenty of water they do not have to actually grow in a pond.

If you have a spot that remains moist and soggy much of the time, it would be ideal for Louisiana irises. They will grow in standing water and thrive at the edges of ponds and pools where their roots are actually in the water. If they are actually growing in water, you do not need to feed or mulch them since they will get what they need from the water. When grown in water, they will grow taller, have larger blooms and will bloom a couple of weeks earlier than those grown in other locations. Another advantage to growing them in water is that iris borers can't live in water and so when they come out of the iris, they drown—"Ha-ha," says Melody Wilhoit. (More about iris borer and other iris problems can be found in section VI, "Pests and Diseases.")

Plant Louisiana iris rhizomes in late summer if they are to be grown in regular garden beds. If you grow them in water, you can plant them at any time except during cold winter weather. Many growers of these irises have the greatest success by growing them in raised beds kept constantly moist. If growing them in raised beds, be sure to establish a regular fertilizer program because they are heavy feeders.

Give them a good spring application of a balanced fertilizer such as 13-13-13, plus lighter applications in the fall, at the end of the year and, in

The Louisiana iris 'Dural White Butterfly' in the photographer's garden. (Photograph by Jim Morris.)

103

the years when you are not transplanting, another light feeding in early spring, about February in the deep South and a few weeks later farther north. Some growers recommend using fertilizers low in nitrogen and high in phosphorus and other nutrients. Others use solutions of liquid fertilizers every couple of weeks from early spring through mid-August. Using a fertilizer that is formulated for azaleas will help keep the soil acidified. Work plenty of composted manure and mulch into the soil and also make regular applications of the same. Composted manure also makes a good topdressing when mixed with straw.

Louisiana irises are quite easy to grow, says Melody. They require no more water than a hybrid tea rose or the lawn. After they are through blooming, she says, they don't need much water because they are somewhat dormant during the heat of summer. They only need enough water then to keep them green at the base of the plant. All of the growth and bud setting are done in the fall. This is when a light feeding and good irrigation are most beneficial.

Mulch during the summer is helpful because the rhizomes tend to work to the surface and can get sunscald. In fact, Louisianas should be mulched all year long. They should be planted about 1 1/2 to 2 inches below the soil surface. More fertilizer is needed if you grow these irises in a boggy area—in such sites you also will have to add to the mulch more often. Further, give them an extra feeding if they are growing in a boggy area because the rapid decomposition that takes place in such sites uses up a lot of nitrogen. Beware of fertilizing if you grow Louisiana irises in ponds because nutrients in the water can cause a heavy bloom of algae, which is something you do not want. Furthermore, Louisiana irises grown in ponds where ducks and/or geese are present may become a feast for the waterfowl.

These irises need sun to perform well. The farther north the garden is, the more sun Louisiana irises should have to flower well. In very hot climates, they will benefit from some afternoon shade. The flowers will last longer if a hot garden site gets afternoon shade.

SPURIA IRISES

Originally from the Mediterranean area of Europe, including the Iberian Peninsula, spurias are beardless or apogon irises that stand out because of their flowers, which have slim standards and falls in the species, and thus resemble the slim graceful flowers of bulbous irises. Currently, botanists recognize about a dozen species plus a number of subspecies in this class of irises.

HISTORY

The irises grouped as spurias are native all around the Mediterranean Sea, from Spain around to North Africa. They also can be found in lesser numbers as far north as eastern England and Denmark, and as far east as Russia, Afghanistan and even western China.

Spuria irises were first introduced into England by Sir Michael Foster in the late nineteenth century. Best known of his introductions was a hybrid called 'Monspur' that proved valuable to spuria hybridizers. Barr and Sons, Ltd., a London nursery, introduced Foster's 'Monspur' and other hybrids.

It wasn't until the 1920s that irisarians began to develop serious programs to improve spuria irises for home gardens. T. A. Washington, the first American breeder of spurias, used 'Monspur' as well as other species in his hybridization programs. The majority of Washington's hybrids inherited the summer-green foliage trait from 'Monspur' and the species *Iris halophila*.

More recently, Eric Nies of Hollywood, California, hybridized in a tight program of 'Monspur' and *I. ochroleuca*. Ben Hager of Stockton, California, has been an outstanding hybridizer for many years. He first won the Nies

Iris spuria, subspecies halophila, is an extremely hardy Russian native.

105

Award for his spuria iris called 'Elixir'. He went on to win the Nies Award many other times, including 1973 for 'Archie Owen', a large, flaring, deep yellow spuria, and 1979 for 'Ila Crawford', a spuria with yellow-and-white ruffled flowers. Hager's hybrids continue to rate highly with growers and gardeners alike.

Although California dominated the spuria iris field for some time, people from other parts of the country have been breeding some excellent spurias in recent years. Dave Niswonger of southeastern Missouri won the Nies Award in 1980 for his 'Buttered Chocolate'. Like Ben Hager, Niswonger has made crosses back to the species spurias in order to get new forms and colors. Hybridizers continue to work to improve a number of qualities in spurias. One effort has been to breed shorter plants with blossoms that are more compact.

Iris hybridizers in the United States have been in the forefront of spuria breeding programs and are responsible for many excellent spuria cultivars in a wide variety of colors. While spuria growing and breeding concentrate in California and the Southwest where the climate is sunny and warm, increasingly spuria fanciers and growers are from places like Missouri and Texas and even states like Minnesota and Montana. The spuria "bug" also has bitten iris growers as far afield as Europe, New Zealand and Australia.

CHARACTERISTICS

Spuria irises will bloom one to two weeks after the tall bearded irises. The flowers and stalks are tough and won't break as easily as those of tall bearded irises. Spurias are wonderful for floral arrangements, each bloom lasting up to three or four days. Cut the flower stalks when the flower buds just begin to show color.

These are among the tallest of irises, most growing as tall as 3 to 4 feet under good growing conditions, and some reaching a height of 5 feet or more. The flower stalk should have at least two buds in its terminal and each branch. Three to four buds per stalk is common, especially on plants with large flowers. Seven flower buds to a stalk is possible but not common. The branching on the spuria flower stalks is sinuous. Leathery leaves, woody rhizomes and wiry roots are characteristic of spuria irises.

Many spuria cultivars are summer dormant, that is, they will stop growing during hot summer months. Spuria iris breeder Dave Niswonger observes that when you go north as far as middle Illinois and farther, most of the spurias

The Spuria iris 'Marilyn Holloway' in the California garden of Marilyn Holloway. (Photograph by Jim Morris.)

The spuria iris 'Kitt Peak' in a Sun City, Arizona garden. (Photograph by Jim Morris.)

stay green all summer and never go dormant. While they are summer dormant, they need no water to supplement scarce summer rains. A few spuria irises, including 'Belise', are classed as "summer-green," that is, they do not go dormant in the summer, but stay green and continue to grow. Summer-green spurias may need extra water if summer rains do not provide enough moisture.

There is a great deal of variation in the number of chromosomes that spuria species have, so much so that it is interesting that many of them can be hybridized. Chromosome numbers range from diploids (original species with the original chromosome number) with a 2n of 16 to a high count of 72. The high chromosome count is found, oddly enough, in a particularly dwarf spuria. There are a number of natural tetraploid spurias, those with twice the normal number of chromosomes, a trait that is significant for greater size, vigor and substance.

107

The trends in spuria iris hybridization are toward shorter plants, flowers with wider petals and flowers without signals, those colored marks that appear in the same locations as the beards of bearded irises. Ben Hager of California, one of several breeders who is working toward shorter spurias, introduced the 19-inch 'Maritima Gem' in 1990. It has cobalt-blue flowers with a pattern of violet lines forming rays that arise in the yellow line signal.

Spurias, though little known to flower arrangers, are wonderful as cut flowers. They also help extend the iris season and make great focal points in the garden. They have been bred in many color variations and patterns, including bicolors, bitones and halos. The promise of a pink spuria is on the horizon, and there already are several rose-colored varieties. Because spuria hybridizers have only been breeding these irises for about eight generations and the bearded irises have been bred for upwards of twenty-five to thirty generations (150 years), the genetic potential of spurias has barely been touched.

CULTURE

Growers and gardeners probably have been underwatering and underfeeding spuria irises, according to Dave Niswonger, who hybridizes spurias in Cape Girardeau, Missouri. They can take more water and fertilizer than tall bearded irises. Growers in the southwestern United States should cut off spurias' water supply and let them go summer dormant after they bloom and summer heat is beginning. In areas farther north and areas with summer rains, spurias will stay green and growing all summer long.

The Niswonger method for planting spurias is to mix 2 gallons of compost into a planting hole that is 12 by 12 by 18 inches. Also mix in a handful of slow-release fertilizer and a handful of superphosphate. Plant *Spuria* rhizomes an inch deeper than tall bearded irises in wet but well-draining spots where tall bearded irises will not thrive. Avoid extra watering during periods of heavy rain and high humidity. This will help the spurias avoid their main enemy, mustard-seed fungus. More about this can be found in section VI, "Pests and Diseases." This is more common in the southwestern part of the country and whenever there is a combination of moisture and hot weather.

Composted barnyard manures are ideal for fertilizing these heavy feeders. If you have no access to manure, you can use a commercial fertilizer such as 10-10-10 or 10-20-10. Plan to plant them in the fall, like most beardless irises, and apply a heavy winter mulch the first year in areas where there usually are subzero temperatures.

An organic soil that does not completely dry out and a site in the full sun are two keys to growing spurias successfully. The richness of the soil will have a considerable effect on the size and bloom production of spuria irises. Iris growers as far north as Wisconsin and Minnesota are having success growing spurias, so growers should not let expectations of severe winter weather discourage them. In more northern regions, spurias will thrive on the sunny southern sides of hills and mountains, while in southern regions they prefer areas of partial shade as well as full sun.

Keep spuria irises well weeded. The combination of weeds, moisture and high temperatures can encourage one of the few disease problems that spurias have—Southern blight, a fungal disease. Since iris borers may be a problem in the Midwest and northern areas, be sure to clean up old foliage and blooms.

Spurias can be lifted and divided in either fall or early spring. Do not let the rhizomes dry out during the process. Spurias generally are shorter the first year after dividing and replanting—in the case of larger plants, there may be a difference of a foot or more between the height of the first-year transplant and that of successive years. There is evidence that storing spuria rhizomes in the refrigerator before replanting them may trigger faster growth and earlier bloom. Dave strongly recommends storing spurias in the refrigerator if you're not ready to plant them when they are received. Dip mature rhizomes in a fungicide and store them in plastic bags in the refrigerator for several weeks to get this response.

These irises also are easy to grow from seed and set seed easily. Spuria seeds germinate better if planted immediately when the pod starts to split. If the spuria seedlings have good growing conditions and are planted early in the growing season, they may bloom the second year after planting. If you don't plan to collect the seed, be sure to cut spent blooms so the plants will not waste energy producing seed. Unless you take the time to make planned cross-pollinations, the seeds would be the results of open pollination by bees and other insects, and thus probably not valuable for growing.

The Japanese iris 'Crystal Halo' in Ladew Garden in
Monkton, Maryland. (Photograph by Riley Probst.)

JAPANESE IRISES

Plate-sized flowers of great and exotic beauty are a hallmark of the Japanese irises (*Iris ensata,* formerly *I. kaempferi*) of today. The flowers can grow to a remarkable 8 to 12 inches in width. Whites, purples, blues and red violets, often with speckling, marbling and dusting effects that lighten the colors, are all in the palette of Japanese irises.

These are plants that originally were native to the quiet waterways, ditches and salt marshes of central and eastern Asia. Skilled hybridizers and growers of Japan have brought these irises to Olympian heights of beauty in form, color and grace.

HISTORY

According to Japanese iris expert and hybridizer Clarence Mahan, there is no mention of the Japanese irises as we know them in historic literature. However, they have been cultivated in Japan for five hundred years. Breeding of these plants did not begin until the early part of the nineteenth century. Although the Japanese irises are newcomers to American gardens when compared to the old and traditional tall bearded irises, they are fast gaining a place in the hearts of our gardeners. This is encouraged by the Society for Japanese Irises (SJI) and its 550 members, which is a section of the American Iris Society. SJI was founded in 1962, more than four decades after the founding of AIS in 1920. During the years ahead, Japanese irises are sure to claim a more important place in American perennial gardens.

Iris kaempferi, *now known as* Iris Ensata, *is the Japanese iris, increasingly popular in American gardens.*

111

For many years, irises and bridges have been associated with Japanese gardens and with each other. A construction and plantings reminiscent of those early garden symbols can be found in the Japanese garden of the Missouri Botanical Garden in St. Louis, where the Yatsuhashi Bridge goes over an iris garden. One legend has it that some Japanese fishermen were lost and sat on the shore beside the water and, missing their wives and families, began to cry, then fell asleep. When they awoke, they saw Japanese irises where their tears had been—the beauty of the irises gave them hope.

For many centuries, Shobu, Japan's sweet flag iris, has been a symbol of good fortune. In Japan, the flowering flag called Hanashobu was until a century ago called Hana-ayame or ayame. The annual Boys' Festival, which takes place on the fifth day of the fifth month, is also known as the Iris Festival. In modern times, both Shobu and Hanashobu are hung at the eaves of homes to ward off evil spirits. The fragrant leaves of the plant called sweet flag (*Acorus japonica*), an aroid and thus no relation to irises, were originally used in these ceremonies and also put in sake and in public baths to scent the water.

Today's Japanese irises all descend from that simple, single violet to purple iris (*I. ensata*) that is native to marshes of Japan, northern China and other regions of eastern Asia. These irises require an acid soil and considerably more soil moisture than the bearded irises, which can't tolerate low, damp places.

Quite probably there originally were a number of variant forms of this iris before agriculture and the other accouterments of civilization replaced the Asaka marshes outside of Tokyo. The Japanese brought this iris into cultivation in the sixteenth century, a time when they were beginning to develop the sophisticated style of gardens for which they are so well known today.

The confusion of scientific names for the Japanese species iris, commonly known as the Japanese water iris, came about centuries ago with the puzzlement between what we know as *I. ensata* and another beardless iris from central and eastern Asia. When *I. kaempferi* was renamed *I. ensata,* that other bearded iris, which had been called *I. ensata,* also had to be renamed and it became *I. lactea.* Plant classification usually helps us understand the relationships among plants, but when looked at from the historical point of view, it can be confusing and sometimes downright mystifying.

The first major hybridizer of Japanese irises was Matsudaira Shoo (1773–1856). His father had collected seed from all the variants of the wild

112

iris he could find and soon, after only three to four generations of iris breeding, he produced a large double-flowered form. By the mid-1800s, Matsudaira Shoo had used collected plants to create hundreds of new varieties. Like other early plant breeders, it is likely that he relied on bees to make the actual crosses.

Even before the Meiji Restoration in 1868, the public began flocking each year to see large gardens of Hanashobu irises. The growing fields at Horikiri about 6 miles east of Tokyo were flooded like rice paddies during the bloom season to enhance their effect. The most famous of these was Kotaka-en. This was when these Japanese irises became known as Edo iris varieties, Edo having been the early name for Tokyo. These irises were prized by members of the wealthy merchant class. After paying a small fee, visitors would sit in one of the viewing pavilions to contemplate the flowers. "Each flower has its own personality," say the Japanese, who value seeing nature through the flower.

The flowers of Edo were noted for their veining, handsome petal edgings and styles in striking, contrasting colors. The blossoms were flat and broad with forms that were not only single, but double and even peonylike with substantial overlapping petals. The single forms have three small, erect standards surrounded by three broad, over-lapping falls. The doubles have six broad and overlapping petals with the standards equal in size to the falls, while the peony types have nine to twelve overlapping falls.

A second major strain of Japanese irises called Ise was developed for pot culture later in the 1800s in the Ise-Matsuzaka district on central Honshu, a district noted for its shrines. These irises have flowers with erect standards that grow at an attractive right angle to the falls. The three falls are broad, overlapping and hang downward. The flowers are in pale colors, often shades of pink. These irises are said to have the grace of a beautiful young woman. They often do not have the strength to grow well under rigorous garden conditions.

A third strain of Japanese irises came about when a feudal lord of Kyushu sent one of his men to study under the hybridizer Matsudaira Shoo in 1833. Some years later, this man, Yoshido-Junnosuko, returned home to the provincial area that is known today as Kumamoto Prefecture. He had with him sixty-four Edo varieties and a breeding frenzy soon occurred. Different groups competed to develop the most beautiful new varieties of irises from the Edo cultivars. They were called Higo varieties after the old name of the province. Each group guarded its Higo irises carefully, not allowing any seeds or plants outside the group. The self-colored Higo irises, originally bred as

The Japanese iris 'Oriental Eye' is a wonderful example of the beauty of the species. (Photograph by Barbara Perry Lawton.)

113

The Japanese iris 'Beautiful Accent' in the Barker/Delmez garden, St. Peters, Missouri. (Photograph by Riley Probst.)

pot plants, traditionally were displayed in front of a golden screen on a bamboo mat spread with a scarlet cloth. Nishida Nebutsume (1862–1938) broke the cult of exclusivity when he began selling and exporting Higo iris plants to Europe and the United States. Edo and Higo irises are the strains most often grown today in the West. Although few Ise varieties are grown in the United States, hybridizers often cross Higo and Edo strains in their quest for handsome new cultivars.

A man named Thomas Hogg was the first to import Japanese irises to the United States. John Lewis Childs of Long Island later owned a collection of Japanese irises. By 1929, Childs had about twenty acres of Japanese irises at his Long Island nursery, Childs's Flower Field. He was a masterful salesman and sold thousands of these irises throughout the United States. Apparently his influence did not last or maybe the gardening public did not receive the right scoop on how to grow Japanese irises. In any case, interest dwindled for the Oriental import and came to center on the tall bearded irises that seemed to be easier to grow in most gardens.

114

Japanese iris breeding in the United States has focused on a few notables. Arthur Hazzard of Kalamazoo, Michigan, began growing these irises with seven varieties he got from the Childs's Nursery on Long Island in 1926. In 1957 when he retired, he began hybridizing and over the following years introduced ninety varieties. A number of these earned the Payne Award, the history of which is described in the next paragraph.

The best known of the hybridizers probably is W. Arlie Payne of Terre Haute, Indiana, who began hybridizing in 1930 with ten Edo varieties. Payne concentrated on improving branching, bud count and plant and flower substance. He worked on linebreeding his Japanese iris strains for some forty years before he began to introduce them to the public. The Payne Award for Japanese irises, the highest award that is solely for Japanese irises, has been established in his memory.

A few years later, Walter Marx of Boring, Oregon, began breeding imported Higo irises. Combining his name with the name of the iris strain, he introduced the resulting plants as Marhigo varieties. He developed a handsome color catalog that surely helped sell his plants. Marx sold his iris cultivars extensively from the late 1940s into the 1970s.

CHARACTERISTICS

The Japanese irises have a great diversity of color patterns. These should be harmonious and clear. They have a variety of textures as well, that quality being determined by the nature of the surface layers of cells of the flower. Japanese iris flowers can have textures that are smooth, rough, waxy, velvety, creped or quilted. In addition, of course, there are the different flower forms.

A Japanese iris show can be bewildering with its burst of colors in unique shades and patterns, often complicated by overlays of other patterns. Some of the color descriptions defy the imagination, such as 'Frostbound', a cultivar described as deep violet with "white wire rims," or others that may have several shades of a color mixed and swirled—described as "marbled."

There are a number of terms commonly used in describing the flowers of Japanese irises. "Sanded" and "brushed" both refer to an impression of scattered sand made by small dark dots and very short broken lines against a pale background. "Washed" refers to an overlay of one or more colors on top of another color. "Splashed" means that one color or combination of colors is laid upon another in irregular spots.

"Mottled" refers to the blotching of different colors as if stained. "Mosaic" is the pattern made by an overlay of a single color over another in a rather coarse pattern. The signal is at the base of each fall in single flowers, in the same location as the beard in bearded irises. Signals are on all six falls in double flowers and can range from pale yellow to deep yellow and even green. "Halo" refers to a narrow band of color that may surround the signal and sharply contrast with the color of the falls.

An excellent place to learn what you can expect from modern Japanese irises is the American Iris Society's *Handbook for Judges and Show Officials*. I turn to this again and again to review the contemporary ideals because of the changing character of many irises over the centuries and even in recent years. Growers show irises in order to display them to the public. In the case of the Japanese irises, there will be several different cultivar classes because of the great diversity of these handsome flowers. They come in not only many colors and color combinations, but also in a variety of color patterns and flower forms. Because of their greater height as compared to most of the bearded irises, they are staged on lower tables so as to be better seen.

The height, branching, flower size and overall plant appearance of Japanese irises depend greatly upon how well they are grown. There are several flower forms and gradations between flower forms. Perfection of form, which counts a great deal in Japanese irises, depends on the aesthetic combinations of the shapes, relative sizes and proportions of the flower parts to each other, and the positions the flower parts hold in relation to each other.

Substance, which is determined by the size, thickness and strength of the tissue structures supporting the plant parts, counts substantially when judging Japanese irises. It is a plant's substance that may make the difference between garden success and garden failure.

A flower that is distinctive in an innovative way that brings a new charm to that flower and sets it apart from other cultivars will gain points for that special quality. This might be a new color, a pleasing texture, a graceful new form, a new color pattern or combinations of these qualities.

The flower stalk and foliage contribute a great deal to a plant's quality. The foliage must be erect, full and of good color. The stalk must be in proportion to the flowers and hold them upright. Overall grace and balance of the plant—foliage, stalk and flowers—will make a Japanese iris a beautiful addition to garden beds and borders.

Look for Japanese iris cultivars that have been bred to hold their flowers in good form for four or five days rather than only two to three days. In choosing Japanese irises for your garden, you will want to look for some of these varieties that offer longer blooming seasons, whatever the reason.

CULTURE

Plant Japanese irises about 3 inches deep in a rich soil that has plenty of organic matter. Fall is the best time to plant or transplant Japanese irises. Although these irises should have plenty of water during the growing season, they do not have to be planted next to ponds or other water features. Within three or more years, depending on their vigor and the number of increases, Japanese irises will become overcrowded. The crown will be approaching the soil surface, stems will be short and blooms will be sparse. That is the sign that it is time to lift, divide and transplant. You can divide and transplant right after the irises flower or in the fall when new root growth begins.

Soil with an acid pH is essential for success in growing Japanese irises. A pH of 5.5 is ideal. Because lime and limy soils are harmful to these acid lovers, do not plant them near fresh mortar work such as newly laid concrete patios, new foundations or newly mortared walls. Bone meal is a definite "no-no" for Japanese iris since this substance releases lime in the soil—indeed, today's bone meal is not very good for anything since so much of the nutrient value has been steamed out of it—better to use superphosphate instead.

To make your soil more acid, add 1 to 3 pounds of agricultural sulfur and plenty of humus or compost to each 100 square feet. Mix it in to a depth of 10 to 12 inches, then let it set for two to three weeks or more, depending upon the weather conditions, and then test the soil pH. Repeat the sulfur amendment if the pH is still too high. Lowering soil pH is more difficult than raising it. The speed with which the sulfur will lower the pH will be greater in warmer weather and in some soils.

Chelated iron products also will increase soil acidity when worked into the soil. Fertilizers formulated for azaleas and rhododendrons often have these materials in them. Japanese irises will indicate when the soil is too basic. The foliage will become chlorotic, that is, it will yellow although leaf veins may remain green. If this happens, you know that you must lower the pH, aiming toward the ideal of 5.5.

Heavy soil will suit these irises very well, so if your soil is light or even sandy in texture, be sure to add plenty of rich compost or humus to meet

Japanese irises grow at the edge of the lake at the Missouri Botanical Garden. (Photograph by Barbara Perry Lawton.)

Japanese iris requirements. They are heavy feeders, so regular additions of organic matter to the soil will encourage vigorous growth. In cool climates, year-round organic mulches with a low pH—ground oak leaves, pine needles, well-rotted or dried manure, bark chips, wood chips or sawdust—will be beneficial in conserving moisture, deterring weeds and furnishing nutrients.

If you use sawdust or wood chips, remember that when these materials decompose, they use nitrogen in the process, so you will have to increase the amount of nitrogen in your fertilizer program. Beware of organic mulches in regions that have hot summers because they may encourage fungal diseases such as rot where there is high heat and humidity.

Some experts have said that manufactured (chemical) fertilizers appear to inhibit the growth of freshly planted Japanese irises. Once the plants have become established and have made a lot of new root growth, manufactured or organic fertilizers are important and will encourage vigorous growth and good flower production. As a general rule, apply fertilizers and organic mulches about three weeks to a month before the bloom season, then again in mid-August, about three to four weeks before the beginning of the fall root-growth period.

Gardeners used to think that Japanese irises could be grown successfully only near permanent bodies of water such as streams, lakes, ponds and bogs. This is not so. On the other hand, these irises do require plenty of moisture during the growing season. In order to produce large flowers, give Japanese irises plenty of water from the time you first see growth in the spring until a month to six weeks after the bloom period.

The plant needs enough moisture and nutrients for the increases, for the development of next spring's buds and for storage of nutrients in the rhizomes. The new plants will become semidormant for the summer months. You should cut back on watering somewhat, but never allow the soil to dry out. An active period of root growth begins again in early fall to store water and nutrients enough to last through winter and the spring burst of growth. Therefore, you should give the plant several heavy waterings during the fall months if rainfall is inadequate. Water if it does not rain for about two weeks, but also check the soil by hand to make sure it does not completely dry out.

Planting times for Japanese irises are in the spring or fall to coincide with the times of most active root growth. Home gardeners will find it easiest to transplant right after bloom when the roots are actively growing. The fall period of root growth is the period when growers will ship Japanese irises.

Plants should arrive well before frost. If you put them directly into the garden, put each plant into a shallow depression in the soil to hold the water, lessen runoff and keep the roots deep in the ground. The rhizomes must be moist if they are to reestablish themselves well.

If they are potted rather than put directly into the garden, Japanese irises can develop a good root system in the pot, then be planted out wherever you wish in the spring. Plunge them into the soil for the winter season to avoid freeze-thaw cycles. If you establish these irises in pots, then you can plant them in the garden at any time of year. Whether Japanese irises are in the soil, in pots plunged into the soil or in pots in plastic pools, protect them from the destructive freezing and thawing cycles that plague the winter season in many parts of our country. In the South where winters are not as taxing, some gardeners grow Japanese irises at the edges of ponds and lakes.

If your climate or soil or both are not suited to growing Japanese irises, try growing them in pots outdoors or indoors, using an acid-type potting soil or mixing up your own highly organic, acidic medium. Rest the pots, which should be 6 inches or more in diameter, in a pan with an inch or so of shallow water so that the pots never dry out. If potted irises are grown outdoors, take them out of water pans and wading pools during winter months and protect them by plunging them into the ground and mulching heavily.

Plan to divide Japanese irises every three to four years. As they grow, the rhizomes rise closer to the soil surface and soon will be high enough in the soil to lack adequate moisture. When the roots don't get enough water, the plant will dwindle and may even disappear. If it looks like this is happening, dig up the plant, pot it temporarily and give it plenty of water, perhaps the plastic-pool treatment to get it growing again.

Growers in areas where the soil and water tend to be highly alkaline will have to keep track of the pH in the soil on a regular basis if they are to have success with the Japanese irises. Regular soil tests for pH should be a normal part of the regimen.

If your soil or climate does not fall within the recommendations for Japanese irises, do not give up. You can grow these beautiful plants in containers or raised beds. Prepare the acid planting medium for the containers or beds, using plenty of sphagnum peat moss or other organic materials with low pH readings.

The Japanese iris 'Hatsukurenai' at the Missouri Botanical Garden. (Photograph by Barbara Perry Lawton.)

119

120   *Iris tectorum, the roof iris, is grown on thatched roofs in China and Japan. Grow in a sunny spot near a fence or wall. (Photograph by Barbara Perry Lawton.)*

SPECIES IRISES

I include the species irises within section IV, which is primarily devoted to beardless or apogon irises, strictly for structural convenience. There are as many bearded iris species and their cultivars as there are beardless iris species. Most of the bearded species have been in cultivation, while many of the beardless species remain less known. Because of that, one is left with the impression that species irises are primarily beardless, but please remember that species irises come in both bearded and beardless forms. Bearded species until recently have usually been included within other classifications. For example, *Iris pumila* is in the miniature dwarf bearded iris (MDB) category.

Species irises can be registered and introduced into the American Iris Society's new classes, Species Iris or Species Iris Crosses (species **X**) just as other irises can be registered within their particular classes. The AIS encourages the registration and introduction of named, selected varieties of iris species. Before AIS established these new classes, many iris species were registered but they were not eligible for AIS garden awards. On the other hand, the species irises have always been eligible for iris show awards. Although one needs only a valid scientific name in order to show a species iris, the further definition of the specimen with a cultivar name is appreciated.

Among these species irises are some well known to American gardeners. Perhaps best known is the American native crested iris, *I. cristata* which is classed within the subsection *Evansia*. This low-growing beauty is found in the wild in the moist woods of the Appalachian and Ozark Mountains.

Iris tectorum, *native to China.*

121

Iris versicolor var. Kermesina is a widespread species iris native to eastern North America. It is a robust garden perennial. (Photograph by Barbara Perry Lawton.)

EVANSIA IRISES

The tiny crested iris, the woodsy North American native and the other irises known as evansias all are distinguished by the frilly crests on their falls. Evansias are native to both eastern Asia and North America. The name "evansia" is in honor of Thomas Evans, who introduced *Iris japonica* to British gardens, and was bestowed on this iris group in 1812.

That frilly crest, a growth out of the central ridge of each evansia fall, is what puts them in the same plant group. They tend to form thick clumps because of their creeping growth habit and vigorously spreading stolons. Other than those traits, this group of about a dozen species of irises is diverse. These irises range in height from only a few inches to well over 3 feet and have flowers, all with a delicately attractive form, that range from small to large.

Iris confusa, an evansia iris from western China, has been cultivated for many years, the well-known W. R. Dykes having been one of the very first Western botanists to obtain seed in 1911. This is a vigorous, clumping iris that has numerous short-lived flowers in shades of white with yellow or purple spots encircling their yellow crests and signals. The 3-foot flower stems are well branched and the flowers open successively well above the broad leaves of the foliage fans. This iris is tender except in the southern states, where it should be grown in partial shade in rich, moist soil.

Japan's roof iris (*Iris tectorum*) is a handsome evansia, one that is hardy and, being low in height, makes a good choice as edging for flowering borders in semishady places. *I. tectorum* comes in blue and white forms. The white-crested blue form is particularly hardy. *I. tectorum* also has plump rhizomes like the common bearded irises and foliage fans of broad but thin-textured leaves.

Irises of the subgenus *Limniris* do not have beards and it is this that separates them from subgenus *Iris*. This group of apogon (beardless) irises includes crested irises (*Lophiris*) and the pond irises (*Limniris*). The *Lophiris* section, known as *Evansia* or crested irises, is best represented in the United States by the native crested iris (*Iris cristata*) of moist woodlands. The section *Limniris,* with all of the irises known as pond irises, includes other beardless irises—such as the Siberian, Pacific Coast, Louisiana, spuria, Japanese and many species irises.

This appears to be a classification of convenience since the crested irises are undoubtedly more closely related to bearded species, as evidenced by a few rare crosses between bearded and crested species. There have been reported crosses between the pond irises (*Limniris*) species and bearded irises but these always have been poorly substantiated or just plain wrong. These are important facts for breeders and gardeners who become interested in the ancestry and relationships of their garden favorites.

Iris cristata, *native to the moist woods of eastern North America, is an ideal choice for shady rock gardens and at the edge of woodlands.*

DWARF BEARDED IRIS SPECIES

The dwarf bearded iris species group includes a number of small irises that are ideal for rock gardens or small garden spaces. Some are easy to grow while others are difficult. They may be easy to grow in one place and impossible in another. In other words, these small plants appear to have a narrow range of environmental tolerances.

Best known of all the dwarf bearded iris species is *Iris pumila.* This iris is often used in hybridization programs leading to cultivars of dwarf bearded irises, those registered and recognized in their own class by the American Iris Society. This species is full of variations in form and color. As the entire plant can be very small, sometimes a *pumila* in bloom will not reach 2 inches in height. The name *pumila* has often been incorrectly applied to hybrid dwarf irises in garden centers. The true species usually is less than 8 inches in height.

Pumilas are native to southeastern Europe and range toward and into Russia as far as the Ural Mountains. They grow in tough lands, in dry grassy plains where the soils are highly basic, high in most nutrients but comparatively low in nitrogen. Their origins are clues to their care in American gardens.

Grow these and other dwarf bearded species irises in rock garden environments. Sometimes a rock garden setting lends itself to planting the dwarf species almost against a vertical rock, a situation that offers great protection from climatic extremes. Bob Pries of High Ridge, Missouri, who has grown many examples of this group of irises over the years, recommends growing them without much water, without much fertilizer and without disturbance. With this kind of hard care, these dwarf species should be long-lived garden plants. As Bob says, the secret to their success is "tough love." He cautions that he is not recommending plant abuse, but too much care at the wrong times can mean certain death.

AN OVERVIEW OF SPECIES IRISES

There are many iris species that will thrive in home gardens in their original genetic state without the benefits of hybridization programs. The original native spurias, Pacific Coast natives, evansias, Siberians, Japanese and other species irises all offer a wide variety of forms, colors, bloom periods and environmental requirements. Not only will many make wonderful garden plants, they also can provide value to hybridizers for backcrosses of hybrids to original species, a practice that may lead to even more new and interesting iris hybrids.

Wildflower fanciers, naturalists and iris breeders alike should all consider growing a few of the species irises that are likely to do well in their own areas. For easy culture, choose species that are from similar environments. If you live in desert country, you will have a hard time growing species from warm moist climates like the Pacific Northwest. The following are just a few of the iris species you might consider.

The vernal iris (*Iris verna*) is similar to the little *I. pumila* except that it doesn't have a beard. This evergreen plant has a clean-cut appearance and is native to the lower Mississippi River Valley, the Carolina dunelands and both the Ozark and Appalachian uplands. Less than 3 inches tall when blooming, the plants will have leaves up to 6 inches in length later in the season. The flowers are a clear violet-blue with an orange stripe down the center of each fall. The rhizomes are compact and spread into large clumps. The vernal iris thrives on rocky, acid woodland soils. In the garden, it requires understory shade and an organic soil that remains moist but not soggy.

Tough and dependable, *Iris versicolor,* commonly called blue flag, is a wonderful plant for wet spots. These irises can tolerate having their roots submerged for most of the growing season. They will grow in just about any kind of soil so long as it is moist. *I. versicolor* is native and widespread in much of eastern North America from Canada to Texas. Growing between 1 and 3 feet in height, this wild iris has arching to erect, stiff leaves. The flowers come in a range of shades from deep blue or blue-purple to lavender and purple to reddish purple—there also are white forms. This iris has the highest chromosome count in the entire genus, with $2n$ being 108. Geneticists have considered this a natural hybrid, a new species that arose from a natural cross between *I. virginica* ($2n=70$) and *I. setosa* var. *interior* ($2n=38$). The resulting hybrid vigor makes this a strong garden plant.

Iris prismatica is another native North American species that grows along the eastern coast from the Carolinas northward to Nova Scotia. Another more vigorous population of *I. prismatica* with the variety name *austrina* grows somewhat inland in Georgia and Tennessee, where it is found in swamps and other moist places not far from the ocean. The spring flowers usually are violet to violet-blue with a thin delicate appearance. There also are white forms. The foliage is thin and tall, reaching up to nearly 3 feet in height. These plants also will form large clumps.

For southern gardens, it would be hard to beat *Iris unguicularis* and its cousins. There are several species in this iris series, none native to North America but rather well-known irises from the northeastern, eastern and southeastern Mediterranean region. The best-known garden form is from Algeria and Tunisia, according to botanist Brian Mathew.

In summary, much of the world's habitat for wild irises is under threat because of construction, conflict and slash-and-burn agriculture. Many iris species have never been brought into cultivation and so remain a mystery as far as their potential value.

Iris setosa, *a species iris that is a good garden plant. This iris is a cold-hardy species that grows naturally in Canada and Alaska.*

At a 1995 international symposium, "Gardening with Iris Species," held at the Missouri Botanical Garden in St. Louis, Dr. Georg Rodionenko of St. Petersburg, Russia, spoke eloquently of the need to investigate the wild species of iris before they are totally lost. In his own part of the world, there are at least a dozen that he knows of which, for one or more reasons, are threatened in the wild.

Rodionenko, here on his first visit to the West, has worked with many of the world's leading iris experts and geneticists during his long and successful scientific career. In 1961, Rodionenko revised the entire *Iris* genus. He also wrote *The Iris,* a book published in 1981 and partially translated into English, which encouraged the cooperation of amateurs and professional botanists in developing the potentials of irises for gardeners throughout his country.

He urged that we all encourage greater cooperation among countries, botanists and horticulturists in collecting and growing the wild irises from as many parts of the world as we can. If we can grow them in our gardens, we can save them from extinction and perhaps one day reintroduce them to their native lands. In addition to preserving these wild plants for their own sake, the value they might have in hybridizing programs focused on developing new garden varieties is inestimable.

Bulbous Irises

XIPHIUM IRISES

The American Iris Society does not place bulbous irises in a separate section. *Xiphiums* (commonly known as Dutch, Spanish and English irises), junos and reticulated irises, all bulbous in form, are registered through the Royal General Bulbgrowers' Society in Hillegom, Holland. This organization is the international authority for bulbous irises. The AIS board of directors has ruled that bulbous irises are not eligible for top iris show awards such as Best of Show since they are not registered with AIS. They are, however, eligible for other iris show awards.

Stars of spring both as cut flowers and in the garden are the tall bulbous irises of the *Xiphium* subgenus. These plants—Spanish iris, English iris and Dutch iris—are tall and slim with flowers of excellent proportion and slim lines. The flower is in shades of white, yellow, blue and violet, with the exception of the English iris, which does not have yellow flower forms.

HISTORY

Originally native to North Africa and western Europe, the subgenus *Xiphium* includes seven species, according to botanist Brian Mathew who wrote the authoritative book *The Iris,* which includes an accepted system of iris classification plus botanical descriptions of irises. Bulbous irises have been in gardens for many centuries, possibly since before the great classical Greek and Roman civilizations. Dioscorides, the Greek physician, wrote of the virtues of the bulbous irises in the first century A.D. John Gerard's 1633 *Herbal* has eleven fine woodcut illustrations of bulbous irises and information on the medicinal uses of these plants.

Iris xiphium.

Massed plantings of Xiphium *irises brighten this Dutch garden.*
(Photograph by Netherlands Flower Bulb Information Center.)

A colorful collection of Dutch irises. (Photograph by Netherland Flower Bulb Information Center.)

Gerard recommends applying the leaves to burns and scalds, and also to inflamed eyes. Decoctions of the root, when mixed with meal made from lupines, were said to clean away freckles. *Xiphium* irises were an ingredient in a concoction that Gerard prescribed to take away the pain of gout.

Mathew classifies *Xiphium*, *Scorpiris* (the juno irises) and *Hermo-dactyloides* (the reticulata irises) as subgenera of the genus *Iris*. While other botanists may have designated the irises in different ways, the Mathew classification makes good sense to me. Where the classification of living things is concerned, you can find many different schools of thought, so you may as well settle on one that makes good sense to you.

Most gardeners grow the modern English and Dutch irises as spring-blooming bulbs. The English iris (*I. latifolia* syn. *I. xiphioides*) has been developed into many selected garden varieties. The Dutch irises, also welcome in the garden as spring-blooming bulbs, were initially hybridized by a Dutch grower from three wild species, as described below.

During the early twentieth century, the Dutch company of Van Tubergen made crosses of two *Xiphiums*, an early large-flowered blue and a large early-blooming yellow. Another Dutch firm, the de Graaffs, combined the same early large-flowered blue *Xiphium* with commercial forms of Spanish irises. The result has been the modern Dutch irises with all the colors of the Spanish irises. They have larger bulbs, stronger growth and taller stems bearing larger flowers. Continued breeding programs are resulting in Dutch irises of even greater vigor with new colors and even earlier bloom times.

CHARACTERISTICS

All of the bulbous irises store nutrients in their bulbs during their growing season. After they flower, their foliage dies back and they go dormant until the following spring when their foliage begins to grow once again. The bulbs are modified stems well adapted for storing the food needed for next season's foliage, flowers and seeds.

The bulbs of these irises are covered with papery or leathery coatings that are not netted, as are the bulbs of the reticulated irises. *Xiphium* bulbs are not large and fleshy like juno bulbs. The comparative characteristics of the bulbs and their coatings are what will help you tell the three types of bulbous iris from one another.

130

The species *Iris xiphium* is one of the ancestors of modern Dutch iris along with *I. filifolia* and *I. tingitana*. The species *I. xiphium* is most often called Spanish iris and grows to 2 feet in height with 4-inch flowers. The leaves are not flat like most irises but almost round or cylindrical. The falls are shaped somewhat like fiddles and the flowers of the species are bluish purple with an orange or yellow patch. They bloom at about the same time as tall bearded irises.

The modern garden hybrids known as Dutch irises come in whites to yellows to blues to purples and are grown extensively as florists' flowers. Commercial growers force the blooms so that they can be available as cut flowers at all times of the year. They are beautiful in the garden, where they are hardy as far north as Zones 6 to 7. The Dutch irises bloom in the late spring, usually just before the first of the tall bearded irises, the exact time being dependent upon the ancestry of the hybrid. Those that have *I. tingitana* as an ancestor are the earliest bloomers of the *Xiphiums*.

The English irises (*I. latifolia* formerly *I. xiphoides*) are descendants of irises native to the Pyrenees Mountains of Spain and France. They were brought to England in the sixteenth century or before and became popular as garden plants. The plant grows to about the same height as the Spanish irises, 2 feet or slightly more with large 4-inch flowers, of violet with a yellow blotch on each fall. There usually are two or three flowers on each strong stem. They bloom after tall bearded and spuria irises, often as late as the Japanese irises.

Selected garden types of English irises have flowers of blue to violet or purple and occasionally white. Unlike Spanish iris (*I. xiphium*), the English iris garden forms do not include a yellow-flowered form. The English irises will thrive in the Pacific Northwest climate. They are more winter-hardy than the Dutch and Spanish irises, but they prefer a climate more like England's than the continental climate of the U.S. interior.

CULTURE

Full sun and a well-draining soil are the most important requirements of these bulbous irises. Plant the bulbs in the fall, from September through November, at a depth of 3 to 4 inches. A light mulch will help protect the bed from severe winter weather. *Xiphiums* are hardy in Zones 5 through 8.

Iris tingitana, one of the Xiphum *irises that is native to northern Africa.*

Unfortunately, the exact identification of bulbs can be difficult, which is not surprising since they are often displayed and sold loose in boxes or bins. They all look alike and often get misplaced. Perhaps it would be wiser to just enjoy a selection, planting them in groups or masses in perennial or mixed garden beds.

If the garden site suits irises of the *Xiphium* subgenus, they will multiply and form thick clumps. You can divide the clumps in the summer when the foliage has turned yellow. Replant them immediately or store them in vermiculite or dry sand until planting time in the fall. A light application of fungicide or milled sphagnum moss (a natural fungicide) will discourage molds.

The best conditions for English irises (*I. latifolia*) are unlike the other species of the subgenus *Xiphium* in that these irises should have cool moist soil throughout their growth cycle. The pH of the soil can be basic to acid. Plant the large bulbs 6 to 8 inches deep. If digging them to divide, be sure to replant them immediately as they will not store easily. Since their leaves do not begin to grow in the fall like the Dutch irises, the English irises are more winter-hardy.

Generally speaking, the English irises are likely to thrive in the Pacific Northwest, although they are difficult to grow in many parts of the United States because of their tendency to get viruses. Dutch irises thrive in the Pacific Northwest, where they are commercially grown. Both the Spanish and Dutch irises will thrive in certain of the mountainous areas in the American Southwest where summers are hot and dry.

Since the bulbs store the nutrients, the carbohydrates made by the green foliage, that foliage should be allowed to grow as long as it will. After the blooming season, the leaves will last awhile, then yellow and wither. Never remove the leaves. If you cut back the foliage while it's still green, you will be preventing the plant from storing nutrients needed to fuel next season's growth.

Plant the bulbs of the English irises in the fall about 5 to 6 inches deep in rich soil that is naturally moist and cool. They prefer a neutral to slightly acid soil, rather than a limy soil, with a pH of over 7.0. Root growth will begin in the fall and the top growth should commence in the spring. The soil should be kept moist until the flowers appear in late spring; then continue to keep the soil moist until the foliage begins to turn yellow and wilt.

If you want to lift and replant the *Xiphium* irises, plan to do that in late

August. Remove offsets and new bulblets only if they break easily. Don't leave the bulbs out of the ground any longer than necessary because they do not store well. If the bulbs are thriving and growing vigorously, there is no need to lift them and replant.

The modern Dutch irises are larger and earlier to bloom than their Spanish ancestors. They are a great addition to the garden, though one might wish for a longer bloom season and less-scanty foliage. Plant groupings of them among daffodils, putting them about 3 to 4 inches deep in a light, well-draining soil. The deeper daffodils won't compete for nutrients, and also provide more foliage. The Dutch irises will bloom after the daffodils.

Since the ancestors of the Dutch irises lived in places with fairly temperate winters, long wet springs and hot dry summers, the modern bulbous plants will thrive in similar sites. Full sun and a light, well-draining soil that is on the sandy side are key to good growth. Thick clumps of a dozen or more bulbs will be far more effective than thinly planted groupings.

If you are growing the Dutch irises for use as cut flowers—and there are few finer for that purpose—do not cut the stems all the way to the ground, but rather leave the lower leaves to help in the development of vigorous new flowering bulbs.

Iris filifolia, *a* Xiphium *iris, is a native to Iberia and northwestern Africa.*

134   *Iris bucharica, shown here in the photographer's garden, is a species of the subgenus* Scorpius, *also known as the juno irises. Juno irises are bulbous irises. (Photograph by Riley Probst.)*

Scorpio (Juno) Irises

While great variety is found among the plants of this group, the distinctive flowers are very much alike, with standards that are much smaller than the falls. The juno standards, which hardly deserve the term "standard" since they are so diminished, usually droop downward but also may appear horizontal. Brian Mathew reports only one juno iris, *Iris cycloglossa*, that has large standards which are quite erect. He says this strange juno looks more like a *Xiphium* iris.

If you wish to grow these unusual irises, the best way to start is to join the American Iris Society and then join the section that is devoted to species irises, the Species Iris Group of North America (SIGNA). These bulbous irises are registered with the Royal General Bulbgrowers' Society and not the American Iris Society, but you will be able to more easily gain information about them through the AIS species iris organization. Members are generous with their time and knowledge. In addition, they can tell you where to get the plants and what is likely to grow vigorously in your part of the country.

HISTORY

There are some fifty-five species in the iris subgenus *Scorpiris,* a group that has plants ranging from midgets with ground-level flowers and very little foliage to some species that are 3 feet or more in height and have large broad leaves. The juno irises are native to central Turkey, the lands at the eastern end of the Mediterranean Sea and through much of central Asia as far as northern Pakistan. Outside of this native territory, there is only one juno species, *Iris planifolia,* that grows in Europe and North Africa.

To the best of my knowledge, most of the juno irises were first collected and named in the nineteenth century. Unlike the tall bearded irises, they have no particular and specific historical importance in either the history of humankind or the history of gardening.

CHARACTERISTICS

You might not even think that juno irises are irises until they bloom. Indeed, botanists have over the years argued about whether juno irises should be included in the genus *Iris* or not. The larger juno plants have foliage that looks rather more like leeks than that of the traditional tall bearded irises. The smaller juno irises have very small and few leaves. The flowers appear nearly at ground level in the center of the foliage. Juno bulbs are large and fleshy compared to the other bulbous irises and they do not have the netted coverings or tunics of the reticulated irises.

The leaves are deeply folded in half lengthwise and are often nested like leek leaves. Just as is the case with the various sizes of bearded irises, the juno irises bloom in a succession that begins with the blooming period of the smallest junos and continues through medium-sized junos with the largest kinds being the last to bloom.

The yearly growing cycle of junos can be read in both aboveground and belowground development. During the time when the foliage and flowers are developing, the thick roots that grow from the bulb will shrink until there are only dried remains. Then, when the flowers have gone by and the leaves are turning yellow and withering, the new bulb forms and new thick roots grow out from the bulb. When planting, be careful of the brittle fleshy roots that grow out from the bulb. If these roots break off, the plant may be set back considerably or even die.

CULTURE

Full sun is a key to growing healthy juno irises. Those junos that are native to the dry steppe and mountainous country of Asia are used to a continental climate, one noted for cold winters with lots of snow and summers that are hot and dry. Juno irises that are originally from warmer Mediterranean areas are tender and can't survive freezing weather. In choosing junos, remember that they are hardy in Zones 8–9 unless otherwise noted.

These irises, after blooming in the spring, prefer to estivate (go dormant) in the summer. The blooming time, which will depend both on the species and on the climate, runs from April through May and even June. Climates that have humid to wet summers are not conducive to the health of juno irises. Some gardeners who are successful in growing junos in such places have had good luck in growing them by cutting off all water, even roofing over the beds to keep rain diverted.

The soil should be that of the native lands, which ranges from sandy to heavy soils depending upon the species. The juno irises do not seem to tolerate acid soils well, preferring soils that are higher in pH such as those that are from regions with limestone bedrock. Gravelly or sandy soil seems to bring success in growing most of the bulbous irises.

If you are growing juno irises in containers, use a soil mix that drains well and beware of overwatering. One key to successful pot culture of junos, according to Alan McMurtrie, a juno expert from Toronto, is to water from the bottom, allowing the potting medium to get nearly dry before rewatering. He also recommends tapering off the watering just prior to the summer when the plants start to die down. Excess moisture is one of the biggest problems in growing junos.

Winter care for junos grown outdoors should include a straw mulch or the equivalent, especially for seedlings. The mulch will help protect the plants from the freeze-thaw cycles that are so destructive. Plants that can stand extreme cold are often severely injured if there are unseasonal warm spells followed by hard cold snaps.

Iris reticulata. (Photograph by Netherland Flower Bulb Information Center.)

RETICULATED IRISES

For very early flowers, the dwarf reticulated irises are a good bet. They get their name from the netted (reticulated) coat that covers their bulbs. Their bright flowers are a welcome sight shortly after winter begins to fade, as early as February or March in some regions.

HISTORY

Some ten species of these small irises, known by their two long basal leaves and by the netted coverings or tunics on their bulbs, have been collected and introduced to the garden world. They were discovered in the geographical area from Israel through Turkey to central Asia. It is quite possible that some of the reticulated irises were brought to Europe after being discovered in the Middle East by Crusaders during the twelfth to fourteenth centuries when western Europeans hoped to win the Holy Land from the Moslems through armed campaigns.

During the Crimean War in the mid-1850s, when control of the holy places in Jerusalem was at stake, Russian forces fought the allied armies of England, France, Turkey and Sardinia. Did some of the soldiers tuck reticulated iris bulbs in their pockets and take them home to western Europe and Great Britain? That is highly likely since one of the known side effects of wars has always been that people and plants get moved around. I have heard that rumored about irises native to the Middle East and western Asia. Unfortunately, I can find no specific supportive information. In any case, this makes a rather romantic story about early distributions of these small irises.

Iris reticulata.

CHARACTERISTICS

The two long leaves are usually four-sided in cross section, but sometimes cylindrical. The leaves of reticulated irises are either four-ribbed or eight-ribbed. These irises die back in the summer after they have completed their blooming and reproductive cycle.

The species *Iris reticulata* is a native of the Caucasus and a good choice for border edges and rock gardens. The flower may be red-purple or blue-purple and blooms very early, along with the early crocuses. The small flowers actually have no stem but rise on a perianth tube up to 6 inches long formed of the standards and falls. The appearance of the flowers is typically irislike.

Another better-known reticulated iris is *I. danfordiae,* a distinctive, small, yellow-flowered iris that is native to Turkey. The *danfordiae* flowers are easily recognized by their very much reduced standards, which appear more like tiny bristles than regular standards.

The *reticulata* iris *I. histrioides* is a good garden choice because of its large, pale blue-purple flowers marked by yellow ridges. This plant is very hardy and the bulbs remain of good productive size. Another native of Asia Minor, this iris sends up a sturdy bloom stalk even before the foliage appears. The leaves grow to a mature length of 16 to 20 inches and are wider than those of other bulbous irises.

CULTURE

Grow these irises in a sandy or gravelly soil. They are good subjects for rock gardening and scree beds. Most are hardy in Zones 6–9 unless otherwise noted. The reticulated irises will thrive on sites that are open, sunny and well draining.

Plant the small bulbs in the fall along paths or in rock gardens. Plant them in masses or large groupings so that the small flowers can make a statement when seen from afar. Up close, they are exquisite, rivaling orchids in their beauty.

If your spring climate is cold and rough, you may prefer to grow the reticulated irises in pots, where they will flower when provided with cool temperatures. Plant several bulbs to a pot. Use a well-draining gravelly or sandy mix, but do not use pure sand or gravel because it will not retain moisture at all.

The reticulated irises can be shy bloomers and may produce many small nonflowering bulblets after the first season in the ground. Normally, the rule of thumb is to plant bulbs at a depth of about three times their height. If you plant the reticulated iris bulbs deeper than that, about 4 to 5 inches deep, the individual bulbs will be more inclined to remain of blooming size.

Pests and Diseases

THE PHILOSOPHY OF
PLANT HEALTH CARE

The current horticultural wisdom on plant health is simple: Healthy plants seldom have severe problems with pests and diseases. This sounds simplistic, but so do other great truths. For too many years, we have used manufactured materials to attempt to solve horticultural problems that are primarily caused by environmental deficiencies.

Gardeners, like others, will likely choose an easy way to do things and we often have taken the short, fast solutions without regard for the longer view. For instance, seeing pests on plants will trigger an obvious response in many people: "Quick, Henry, the Flit!" Many people want to zap every bug they see in the garden. As a master gardener, I run into this response all the time in trying to help people solve their gardening problems. They see pests and immediately run to get a can of insecticide.

The problem with that is, first of all, the pests may be a symptom rather than a primary problem. They may be on the plant because it is weak and not thriving. Secondly, the insecticide may be like using a sledge-hammer to kill a fly—it may be more powerful, more poisonous than needed. Also, using pesticides with a generous hand will kill beneficial insects and other creatures that would control the pests if left to their own devices. Finally, most people do not make the effort and take the time to read the labels of the chemicals they use in their gardens. That is a dangerous practice because there definitely are garden pesticides and other chemicals for garden use that are harmful to people, pets, fish and other living things if used in the wrong way.

While I am not a rabidly organic gardener, I do prefer conservative gardening methods that save both time and money while resulting in vigorous plants. Conservative methods are those of our grandparents and great-grandparents, who grew plants very well without the modern wonders that promise to zap our way to gardening success.

A number of factors work together to make plants healthy. Perhaps one of the most important principles is to do enough research to be able to place the right plant in a given place. You can't put a woodland fern in a desert setting any more than you can place a cactus in a woodland garden. These are obvious cases of wrong plants in the wrong places.

For iris-lovers, growing the right plant in the right spot will mean that there are irises that you shouldn't even try to grow. If you live in the Northeast, don't even think of trying to grow aril irises, for instance. If you live in tropical Florida, just look at the pretty pictures of tall bearded irises. If you live in the Great Lakes region, you can forget about growing those beautiful Pacific Coast irises. Of course, there will always be people who try to grow the difficult things, but do not count me in that group.

There are plenty of gorgeous irises for just about any part of our country; therefore, if you want to grow the easy way, do some research to discover what irises grow best in your specific region. There always will be those exceptional gardeners who find ways to grow plants out of their normal ranges with success. My hat is off to them but I would rather grow what is best suited for my climate and soil.

If the research part seems overwhelming, do it the easy way. Just visit the nearest public garden or botanical garden during the spring when most irises bloom and make notes of the labeled irises you like, or ask the gardeners if there are no labels. The second easy way to research what irises will thrive in your neck of the woods is to join the local iris society and go to a few meetings. Many spring meetings include tours of member gardens and other meetings include slide shows and solid information on growing irises in your location. Most members are generous with their time and knowledge with anyone who has serious interest in growing irises.

Unfortunately, the environmental deficiencies of garden sites are often very subtle, making them difficult to analyze when trying to make choices in ornamental plants. Increasingly, horticulturists and plant physiologists are discovering that the microscopic life in soils is extremely important to the growth of green plants. Whereas some gardeners mistakenly believe that the garden environment, including the soil, is full of things harmful to plants, the fact is that most of the plant and animal life in the soil is actually beneficial.

Every year there are advances in soil science that stress the importance of microbial life to green plants. There are some experts who say that green plants could not exist without certain soil fungi. Clearly we have only scratched the surface of soil science, if you'll forgive a dreadful pun. We do know that about half of the volume of soil usually consists of air spaces between crumbs of soil. Those crumbs of soil are partly mineral particles and partly organic matter.

The texture of the soil—sand, silt or clay—depends upon the size of the mineral particles, with clay having the smallest particles and sand having the largest. The sizes of silt particles fall in between clay and sand. You can't change the texture of your soil, but you can change the structure of the soil by adding organic matter that will cause the soil to form bigger irregular crumbs of soil. The irregularities of the soil crumbs allow good air and water circulation needed by plant roots.

Plants grown in soil with an appreciable amount of organic matter are able to thrive under a wider range of growing conditions. This is because organic soils conserve moisture, buffer temperature extremes, drain well, contain plenty of oxygen and have a lot of microbial life known to benefit plant metabolism. Although there are some irises that need to be grown in sandy desert-type soils, most will benefit from soils with organic matter.

The water film on the soil crumbs of moist soil is necessary for plant growth since it serves the circulatory system and contains nutrients in solution. The nutrients must be in solution for the plant roots to take them up. The pH of the soil is important in order for plant nutrients to be in solution. A pH that is too high (alkaline) or too low (acid) will cause plant nutrients to be locked up into chemical salts that are not soluble.

There are earthworms and other similarly sized creatures that tunnel through the soil, aerating it and improving its structure through the addition of their castings. There are also mite-sized creatures that live in the air spaces between soil crumbs and microscopic protozoan bits of life that live in the water film. Increasingly, there are studies showing that much of this soil life benefits plants.

Failure to thrive is common with plants that lack the right exposure, light, soil, soil pH, temperature, moisture or nutrients. Cultural diseases include all conditions caused by environmental problems. Symptoms may include discolored or spotted leaves, blighted blooms, limp foliage and flower stems, or just a general puny look. You should learn the look of healthy irises in order to be able to diagnose plant problems when they occur.

Blighted or aborted blossoms are examples of physiological disorders that can be caused by many environmental factors, including low light intensity, lack of water and even temperatures that are too high. Wilting stems may be caused by a calcium deficiency. Scorched leaves can be caused by frost or by hot dry winds and too little rain.

Another environmental factor that can be devastating to irises of all kinds is the damage caused by herbicides. While some have thought that you could apply weed retardants to established iris beds, others have discovered, to their dismay, that these chemicals can seriously injure or even kill irises. Beware of ever applying any herbicide when there is a breeze. Be sure to read all of the small print on the label. Follow directions carefully. Better yet, develop a schedule of regular hand-weeding and mulching (except over bearded iris rhizomes) to keep weeds to a minimum.

When growing irises, as when growing most other plants, a key to success is to have your garden environment closely match that of the irises' native habitat. Irises that were originally collected from places with hot, dry summers are unlikely to do well in places with muggy, rainy summers. In the chapters about the many different types of irises, the parts that tell about culture are in a sense little more than a description of the irises' native lands. Adding organic matter to the soil will improve its overall structure, which means that it will conserve moisture, moderate the temperature, improve air circulation within the soil and increase the nutrient value. Mulching is another good conservative garden practice, although you must not cover the rhizomes of bearded irises. Mulches with shredded bark or whatever other organic materials are easily available in your region. Mulch only the surrounding soil, keeping the mulch away from the iris rhizomes.

Regular application of mulches also will help conserve soil moisture and moderate soil temperature. In addition, the mulch will prevent the growth of many weeds and those that do grow will be easier to pull when they grow in the mulch. Remember, though, that when mulches break down, they deplete nitrogen in the soil, as nitrogen is a major requirement for the decomposition of organic matter. Shredded bark mulches will last longer and therefore

145

deplete soil nitrogen more slowly than mulches consisting mainly of sawdust or wood chips.

If you are in doubt about the quality of your garden soil, be sure to have a soil test made by your county's horticultural extension service. The county agent will give you instructions on how to take a soil sample. The results will tell you if and what you need to add to bring your soil up to flower garden requirements. The cost of a simple soil analysis—one that checks nitrogen, phosphorus, potassium and organic matter—will probably be about $15, a small price to pay for the information.

In dealing with pests and diseases, the principles of integrated pest management (IPM) can easily be applied to the culture of irises. IPM was developed for commercial agricultural pest control so that farmers and other growers could cut down on costs, time and any negative effects of modern pesticides. Before IPM became an accepted conservation practice, farmers often sprayed pesticides according to the calendar rather than according to what pests had appeared.

The IPM technique calls for, first of all, identifying the pest or disease and learning about its biology and natural enemies. Then the grower monitors the disease or pest population through observation or traps, or both. The grower should observe the level of injury to the plants and establish a tolerable threshold of injury.

When these steps have been taken, the grower should use cultural, biological and mechanical methods to control unacceptable levels of pest populations. Note that the operative word is "control" and not "get rid of." Only if conservative methods fail should you consider using stronger chemical controls. And be sure to thoroughly read the labels before using any product. Environmentally conscious pest management programs are gaining headway with all growers and gardeners.

There are a number of environmentally sound pest control methods. When used in combination, they will help you grow healthier plants and, as I said earlier, healthy plants have fewer problems. Easiest of all is to handpick or squash pests as soon as you notice them. Spray pests such as aphids or spider mites off the plants with a hard fine spray of water from the garden hose.

Get and apply natural predators that will consume pests—lacewings, ladybugs and praying mantises are among the better-known types. Use microbial organisms such as *Bacillus thuringiensis* (BT) that make certain pests sick. BT will sicken and kill the larvae of many butterflies, including such pests as the cabbageworm. Use disease-resistant varieties—grow plants that are well adapted to your climate and region. Keep a clean and tidy garden. This is very important when growing irises because major pests, including iris borers, and diseases may live in old iris leaves and other ground litter. Destroy diseased plants. Maintain healthy fertile soil that has abundant soil life.

Other garden practices that will help your plants grow vigorously and beautifully include purchasing and planting only top-quality, healthy plants. Do not overcrowd plants. Give them enough room for there to be good air circulation, another major requirement for growing irises successfully. Water in the mornings so that the foliage will not go into the night wet, a condition that encourages the development of fungal diseases. See that plants get the right amount of moisture and nutrients for the particular type or species. Remove diseased and dead plant parts from the garden.

Good gardening habits and the knowledge of disease and pest cycles will give you a distinct advantage in growing healthy, productive irises. You will do far better with your irises if you grow only those types that are known to thrive in your region. Just remember that the right plant in the right place is an important factor in growing healthy plants.

In the following two chapters, I describe a few of the most common pests and diseases of irises, and provide conservative advice on controlling or preventing them. These days, most gardeners prefer to use the most conservative methods rather than immediately looking for a way to chemically zap the pest or pathogen. If you choose to use chemical controls, you can find them at any garden center. Use them wisely and be sure to read the directions before using them. Even if you use these manufactured products, be sure to diagnose your garden problem first. Then you will have the knowledge needed to look for the product that is labeled for that particular problem.

PESTS

Although irises are noteworthy for their general pest resistance, there are a few pests, mostly insects, that will attack many of the irises. Descriptions of the pests, their life cycles and the damage they do will help you check for possible identifications when you investigate situations that look like pest damage. Some of the most common are listed below along with appropriate conservative controls. The insect pests of irises are listed first, then the pests belonging to different animal classes are described.

INSECT PESTS OF IRISES

APHIDS

Aphids of many species are common throughout the garden and the woods and fields beyond. There are over 4,000 aphid species in the world and most of them feed only on a few closely related plants. Adult aphids are tiny—no more than about 1/8 inch long—pear-shaped and equipped with long antennae. Often called plant lice, they come in several colors: green, yellow, red, brown, gray and black. The different stages of aphids may be different colors. They have two tubercles (tubelike organs) projecting backward from the top rear of the abdomen. Some have wings and others don't, depending on environment and the species. When food runs short or other conditions are not right for aphids, the females produce more winged aphids to fly away and colonize better possible sites.

Aphids overwinter as eggs in protected spots on plants. In the spring, the unfertilized females that hatched from eggs give birth to live young that are all female. This is an example of parthenogenic reproduction. Aphids have piercing, sucking mouthparts that they use to suck the plant juices from foliage. They excrete a sugary substance called honeydew that is sweet and attracts ants. In fact, honeydew is so attractive to ants that the ants may care for aphids, tending them as we would tend sheep. The honeydew makes the plants sticky, and it also supports the growth of a black sooty mold that is both unsightly and can cut back on plants' manufacture of carbohydrates if it covers large areas.

When there is extensive aphid damage on foliage, it can look like a pale rash where the aphids have sucked out the plant juices, including some of the green chloroplasts from the cells. Extreme aphid damage may also cause leaves to curl or bend in an unnatural way because the side of the leaf with the most damage has lost the most fluid, and so is less turgid than the other side. The unequal pressures cause the leaves to curl.

Primary aphid damage is seldom a big problem to iris growers. The greater danger is that some common aphids are carriers for iris mosaic virus. When they feed on the iris foliage, they can inject the virus into the plant. This is why it is a good garden practice to monitor for aphids.

CONTROL—Aphids are comparatively simple to control. The easiest way to get them off plants is to spray them in the morning (to avoid wet foliage at night that can encourage fungal disease) with a hard fine spray of water to knock them from the plants. Make sure the spray reaches insects underneath plant parts as well as those in sight. Repeat as needed. Often, this is the only treatment that is needed when you have just a few irises. If aphids persist, a spray of ultrafine horticultural oil or insecticidal soap should take care of the problem. These substances are safe and almost as conservative as spraying with the garden hose. Remember, though, to be sure that you spray all sides of the foliage to reach the majority of aphids.

There also are direct biological controls that involve aphid predators such as ladybugs, green lacewings and aphid-eating gall midges. Be sure to read the instructions or get information from your organic-garden supplier before you use these biological controls. Other conservative substances are pyrethrum or pyrethrins (the former is the natural substance found in a kind of composite plant and the latter are manufactured replicas of pyrethrum); use according to directions if the most conservative methods do not result in good aphid control. Be sure to aim at the pesky aphids and not broadcast insecticidal soap, pyrethrum or pyrethrins, because they also will kill beneficial insects.

IRIS BORER

The iris borer (*Macronoctua onusta*) is without doubt the most prevalent pest that afflicts irises. Fortunately, not all of the United States is afflicted with the iris borer. Its normal range is from Maine and eastern Canada, south to the District of Columbia and west as far as Iowa. Its southern limit is not usually south of Tennessee. The iris borer is rare outside of these limits. These borers are especially common in the Midwest above the Mason-Dixon Line.

This serious iris pest is the larva of a small moth. The larva's body is white shading toward pale pink to light red on the dorsal side, and its head is brown. The moth is less than an inch long with a wingspan of 1.6 to 2.25 inches. The body of this moth is dark at the thorax, grading to lighter brown on the abdomen. The front pair of wings have fine black lines on a dull brown background. The hind wings are tan at the outer edges, shading to off-white near the body. Overall, the borer moth has a plump and furry appearance and, like most moths, generally rests with its wings folded back along the body. The sexes are similar in appearance.

There may be as many as three to four different hatches of iris borers each year, beginning in early spring when the tall bearded iris foliage is only 6 to 8 inches tall. These hatches appear to be a function of the weather. If spring is cold and wet, borers will hatch later than they would in a warm spring.

You will more likely see the signs of the iris borer on iris plants beginning in late spring, usually May and June. At first, look for tiny pinholes made in the leaves near the base of the leaves or wherever the eggs were laid. Then look for young leaves that are notched or have ragged edges. Borers may start at the bottom of the foliage or on the outer leaves of the foliage fans, but then they always go toward the top of the fan and to the central, most tender and freshest leaf. They may leave a little silver trail that you can see in the right light.

You may find one or more borers in the creases of the leaves just outside of the central leaf. Although the larvae are cannibalistic, when there is plenty of tender foliage, you may find several on one fan. They will work their way down through the leaves and into the rhizomes. They may eat their way through several rhizomes before they pupate.

150

Later in the season, during the summer months of July and August, you are likely to find small piles of frass (insect excrement) or "sawdust" around the base of the iris plants. By this time, the borers may have hollowed out the rhizome.

In mid- to late summer, the larva is about 1 to an 1 1/2 inches in length. If the iris plant is heavily infested, you may also see that the foliage at the base of the plant looks watery and slimy, or you may see plant juices oozing from the edges of young leaves. Iris experts explain that iris borers are omnivorous and eat not only iris tissues but also each other. For that reason, you usually will find only one borer per rhizome.

If you are going to control the iris borer, it is important to be able to identify it and equally important to know its life cycle. The eggs are usually laid by the moth from mid-September through October. The parent moths mate in the leaves and ground debris soon after they hatch from the pupae that developed in the soil. The females lay as many as two hundred eggs in groups of twenty-five to thirty in sheltered places on old flower stalks or leaves and in rhizome cracks or ground debris. The moths are weak flyers that may be found on dark gloomy days or at dusk hovering around irises. Iris borer moths evidently are not attracted to light and so are seldom seen even when they are most active: at night during late September to mid-November. There will be more moths and thus more iris borers in beds where the irises are thickly planted.

Some of the shiny brown pupae may overwinter as well, in which case the adults will emerge, mate and lay eggs that hatch later than those from overwintering eggs. Once the larvae hatch, they climb up the iris foliage and chew small holes in the leaves. Then in a few days, they will begin tunneling into the leaf. They work their way toward the base of the leaf sheathes for about a week. When they gnaw the edges of the new leaves, the leaves bleed, and this is what causes the watery, slimy appearance at the base of the plant.

The larvae grow larger as they feed and soon begin to eat larger pieces from the edges of center leaves, giving them a jagged look. As they feed and grow, the larvae work their way to the base of the iris plant, where they tunnel into the rhizomes from within the leaf sheaths. They eat the rhizome tissue, often hollowing the rhizome out so that it is nothing but a shell.

Borers will also eat their way into bloom stalks and even into the flowers. They are especially likely to do that in Louisiana irises. Louisianas are their irises of choice, with tall bearded irises second and Siberian irises third. When borers get into Siberians, it can be a mess resulting in the loss of the whole clump. Siberian iris foliage is tough and it is more difficult to find the borers because those tender central leaves are more hidden.

CONTROL—To avoid getting borers in Siberian irises, a common practice in regions from the Midwest north is to burn the foliage on a calm, dry day in January or February. If you can't burn the foliage, at least cut it very short after it browns out.

In some cases, where there are densely growing rhizomes, the larvae will work their way underground from rhizome to rhizome. That makes diagnosis difficult since you cannot detect the borers aboveground. When the larvae are mature, they pupate in the soil near the irises that have fed them. If you suspect severe borer damage in your iris rhizomes, the evidence will be clear with a little practice. Search for and destroy the larvae, using a pocket knife to get into the rhizomes if necessary. If they have eaten a lot of the rhizome, the plant probably wouldn't have lived anyway. Clearly, one control is not to let iris rhizomes become so crowded that they are touching.

If you are taking care of your irises pretty well and removing the dead foliage in very early spring, that will remove most of the iris borer eggs and thus prevent most of the larvae from hatching in your garden. Monitor your irises well during the spring months to find the larvae that remain. When the borers have gone into the central leaf, you often can run your fingers down that center lead and pinch out borers. Finding the grubs and destroying them will keep plant damage to a minimum. Tear the tip off a leaf where you found a borer so you can keep track of the places you found larvae.

Removing old iris foliage and other debris from the garden before spring arrives is a good way to eliminate iris borer eggs before they hatch. Do not compost iris foliage because of the danger of nurturing iris borers and other pests. In addition to keeping your garden clean, carefully inspect all new plants. A good idea is to soak new plants in a dilute solution of household chlorine bleach (one part bleach to nine parts water), then let them dry out. That should get rid of borers, fungal diseases and other problems.

Some iris growers do nothing at all about borers that get into their irises, but this can be risky since borers can destroy entire iris beds if ignored. In the past, many irisarians used heavy-duty pesticides in their efforts to eradicate iris borers, but the current move is far more conservative and aims to avoid the use of chemicals that may have undesirable side effects.

The American Iris Society Foundation funded a 1995 study at Maryland University on the control of iris borers using insect pathogenic methods. Perhaps we will have some valuable new controls for this pest when the results of this study become available.

Genetic intervention has resulted in potatoes that repel potato beetles because of a special gene that has been inserted into their chromosomes. In the future, perhaps scientists will insert a gene into irises that will make them repel iris borers. Certainly, if you live in an area known for heavy iris borer infestations, you might be willing to pay a little extra for such plants.

IRIS WEEVIL

Those who breed beardless irises may be troubled by the iris weevil (*Mononychus vulpeculus*). The adult female of this insect, sometimes called the iris snout beetle because of its long-nosed appearance, pierces the ovary of the apogon iris flower and lays its eggs within. It prefers to lay its eggs in Siberian irises and *Iris versicolor*, the large blue flag that is native to the northeastern quadrant of the United States. Like other insects, the life cycle of the iris weevil consists of four stages—egg, larva, pupa and adult. There is a single generation each year.

The egg hatches into a short, fat, legless larva that is slightly curved. The larva pupates within the seedpods and, when the seedpod ripens and splits open, the adult emerges. The adult beetle is about 1/5 inch long. It is black on the dorsal surface and the body underneath the wing covers is covered with whitish to yellowish scales.

The adult weevil feeds on flower blossoms, making holes as it goes, and also feeds on seeds and other seedpod tissue by pushing its snout into seedpods. This naturally causes the pod to have irregular corky scars. For some strange reason, this insect pest prefers blue varieties of late TB irises and will avoid white Siberian irises. This insect overwinters in the ground debris near iris plants as an adult, and the iris weevil is common over the eastern half of the country from Maine and Wisconsin south to Georgia.

CONTROL—The easiest way to control iris weevils is to remove and destroy the seed capsules of Siberian irises and *I. versicolor*. Those who breed these

153

irises can prevent weevil damage by bagging the seedpods with cheesecloth or the equivalent. Old nylon stockings provide a good fabric for bagging seedpods. Again, it is important to regularly inspect your irises for signs of pest damage.

SCALE

Scales are a minor pest of irises. There are many species of scale insects and some are serious pests of both ornamental and useful plants. Scale insects are small, about the same size as aphids, and have piercing/sucking mouthparts so that they can feed on plant sap. When these pests occur in large numbers, they can cause the host plants to decline or even die.

There are two main groups of scale insects, the soft scales and the armored scales. Female soft scales move around as immature crawlers, then settle in one feeding spot and are covered by cottony or smooth covers, retaining their legs and antennae. Soft scales, like aphids, excrete honeydew and often attract ants and sooty mold fungus.

Female armored scales lose their legs one to two days after hatching, settle in permanent feeding spots and develop a hard shell that usually is separate from the insect's body. The females breed and lay eggs under the shell. Protected by their shells, the scales are protected from the environment and from sprays. Only in the crawling stage are these insect pests vulnerable to spray controls.

The male scale insects resemble tiny wasps and usually live only long enough to mate. Some scale species reproduce by parthenogenesis, not needing the male insect to reproduce. The offspring of these are, of course, all female.

CONTROL—Fortunately, there are usually enough natural controls, predators of the scale insects, to prevent unusual population buildups. Predators of scale insects include ladybugs, also known as ladybird beetles, and parasitic wasps. These can be bought in increasing numbers of garden centers. Using an insecticide is not recommended for controlling scale since the insecticide will also kill the scale predators and the result will be a buildup in scale population.

Ultrafine horticultural oils applied according to instructions are increasingly being targeted toward scale control. If only a plant or two are severely infested with scale, the easiest thing to do is to destroy those plants. If only a few scales are present, carefully inspect all the foliage and destroy the scale insects by hand, firmly rubbing them off the leaves. Some prefer to use a cotton swab dipped in alcohol to kill scale insects.

THRIPS

Iris thrips (*Bregmatothrips iridis*) are small insects with the usual four-stage insect life cycle. They sometimes will attack irises and then, most often, the Japanese irises. Less than $1/20$ inch in length, they are nonetheless easily recognized by the fringe that grows on the margins of both sets of wings. While some thrips are carnivorous and feed on insects and mites, others feed on plants, using their rasping mouthparts to scrape plant tissue from leaf and flower surfaces. While this is unsightly, thrips will not kill irises. The scars they leave look like windburn.

CONTROL—Thrips usually are fairly easy to control. In most cases, you can knock them down with a hard fine spray of water just as you would aphids. Insecticidal soap and ultrafine horticultural oil are two conservative controls for thrips. There also are predatory mites that are commercially available and recommended to control thrips.

VERBENA BUD MOTH

Next to the iris borer, the verbena bud moth (*Endothenia hebesana*) is the most serious iris pest. This pest destroys iris seeds while they are in the ripening pods and so are a particular threat to iris breeders. They are likely to be found on any iris, as they have many host plants including verbenas, gold-enrods, snapdragons, penstemons and physostegias. You can differentiate their signs from those of iris weevils by the silken coatings they make on their tunnels between seed capsules. Look for a small hole in the seedpod. There likely will be frass below the hole and a piece of the pupal skin protruding from the hole.

Egg, larva, pupa and adult are the typical four stages that the verbena bud moth, like all insects, goes through. The entire cycle takes forty-five days. Unfortunately, there are four or more broods of verbena bud moths each year and the moths can overwinter as either larvae or pupae. The eggs, laid on the surface of the seedpod, are very tiny and white in color, turning a little darker just before hatching. The small larva, found on or in the seedpod, is pale, hairy and almost transparent with a dark head. The larva is only 1/2 inch in length when it pupates within a shiny brown silk cocoon. After the adult moth emerges, it crawls out of the seedpod, leaving the pupal skin sticking out of the hole.

The adult verbena bud moth is only 1/2 inch long and triangular in shape when at rest. It has a buff-colored head, dark eyes and short antennae. The abdomen is gray and the forewings are gray and brown with purple-tinted metallic markings. The hind wings are paler brown, becoming darker toward the rear.

CONTROL—Removing and destroying seedpods is the best control for iris growers. Since there are many host plants, also watch for signs of damage on other flowering garden plants. Deadheading flowers when they fade to prevent seed production will remove places for the verbena bud moth to breed and, in many garden perennials, also encourage reblooming. Breeders who are hoping for seed production will have to bag the desired seedpods with cheesecloth, nylon from stockings or the equivalent.

OTHER PESTS OF IRISES
NEMATODES

Nematodes, also known as roundworms or eelworms, are microscopic organisms that live in the soil. There are many species of both good and bad nematodes from a gardener's point of view. There are beneficial nematodes that are used effectively to get rid of lawn and garden grubs. There also are bad nematodes that attack plants, sucking the nutrient-laden plant juices from small plant roots. Nematodes, because of their microscopic size, are often considered a disease rather than a pest.

There are few nematode problems in most of the western part of the United States, where dry soil and severe winter temperatures are not hospitable for these pests. However, harmful nematodes are common in some soils of warm southern regions and some parts of California. Nematodes are more of a problem where winter temperatures are mild and the soils are sandy and well draining.

If you are in a part of the country that has nematodes—check with your county extension agent if you are in doubt—you should be suspicious if some of your irises are stunted and have pale, yellow-green leaves with brown tips. Dig such a plant up and study the roots, looking for swollen nodules near the root tips.

CONTROL—Nematode control is difficult at best. Since it is well known that water-stressed plants are more likely to have nematode damage, increasing the organic content of sandy soils is one good way to avoid water stress since that will increase the water-holding capacity of the soil. Regular irrigation is another way to avoid drought stress. Avoid the drought-flood cycles of watering and you will lessen the chances of nematode damage.

For years, an old wives' tale has been that growing marigolds will get rid of nematodes in your soil. Finally, someone did some studies on this and found that, if you grow smelly marigolds in a plot and then cultivate them into the soil, they *will* get rid of nematodes. Just growing any marigolds around a plot will not do a thing except give you gold and yellow flowers.

In the future, there may be biological controls that will attack and kill damaging nematodes but, to my knowledge, none has been proven as yet. Some common possible beneficial biological controls include fungi, bacteria, other nematodes and some soil-dwelling insects.

SLUGS AND SNAILS

Slugs are closely related to snails and both are gastropods in the phylum Mollusca. Both slugs and snails may eat the foliage of a wide variety of plant species, sometimes including irises. The worst part of the country for snail damage is California, where the introduced snails are rampant. Too bad they can't be turned into an expensive delicacy and sold as escargot. At least forty species of slugs are common in many parts of the country.

Both slugs and snails lay masses of eggs in debris, soil cracks and in moist, shady places under plants. They thrive in moist places and are most active at night and sometimes on dark gloomy days. They avoid hot, sunny situations and other drying conditions. During daylight hours, you can find them in sheltered places, under debris or in any place that is dark and moist. They are not active when the temperature is under 50 degrees F.

CONTROL—An easy and successful control is to handpick snails and slugs from your irises at night when they are most active. Take a flashlight and a container with a weak alcohol solution (3 to 5 percent) to anesthetize the pests. Begin a couple of hours after sunset when they are at their most active. Remove them from other nearby plants as well. Combine handpicking with some other controls to successfully protect your irises.

Amphibians and reptiles are fond of these pests. Be sure to protect those that come to your garden. If you are in the country, you should know that ducks are fond of slugs and snails. Barriers of copper foil are excellent repellents since slugs and snails are sensitive to some metal ions. The copper-foil technique is especially effective in raised beds. Diatomaceous earth, wood ashes and boric acid crystals strewn around plants will protect plants from snails and slugs, but will have to be replaced after rains.

Snail and slug traps are another good way to control snails and slugs. Place inverted grapefruit rinds or moist trap-boards of old wood on the ground in the garden where you see signs of the pests, such as holes in foliage. Be sure to check underneath these traps every morning to remove and destroy the pests. The traditional beer-baited saucers are fine but not reliable controls when used alone. The problem is that, if young tender foliage is nearby, the pests prefer it.

There are snail baits but they may be hazardous. You should be very careful about using baits where children and pets may be around and can get exposed to the poison.

VOLES

Meadow mice or voles (*Microtus* species) can injure irises by chewing on the foliage or the roots. When this happens, it seems to be most common on Japanese and Louisiana irises. Voles seem to like to eat anything green, including plants and also bulbs, rhizomes and tubers. They are rodents that are related to mice; they look like short-tailed mice.

They actively reproduce throughout the year and each litter typically has three to six young. They mature in a little over six weeks and have a short life span, usually under a year. Vole populations may fluctuate greatly from year to year. For instance, last year in Missouri, practically all the gardeners I know were complaining of vole damage in their gardens.

Voles often travel in mole runs, which fools gardeners into thinking that the moles have done the damage. Although moles are totally carnivorous and eat only grubs, earthworms and other animal life, not plants, they may

158

disturb iris growth by tunneling under plants and disturbing the roots. Voles also make their own system of underground runs and surface paths that they clear and mow. Several voles usually run in one "highway" system.

CONTROL—One of the best controls for voles is the household cat. Owls, weasels and the larger snakes also are fond of eating voles. Controls are otherwise difficult. A sure control is to use wire meshing with spaces no bigger than $1/4$ inch to surround garden beds, sinking it 6 inches into the soil and leaving it several inches high on top of the soil surface.

Mechanical mousetraps placed lengthwise along runways and aimed away from the garden can be effective. If you place them correctly, you won't even have to use bait. Hot pepper sauce diluted with water and sprayed on the plants will keep any animals from eating anything, but it washes off in rain and must be replaced.

If voles are running in mole runs, you can discourage or get rid of both by putting dry ice into the tunnels and sealing up every opening you can find. Dry ice reverts to carbon dioxide and, according to some iris experts, both moles and voles will go to sleep peacefully.

There also are poison rodent baits. If you choose to use them, read the directions carefully and use as directed. Although some rodent baits are specific poisons for rodents, I still recommend that you place the baits where they will not be accessible to children and pets.

BACTERIAL, FUNGAL AND VIRAL DISEASES

While irises are generally quite free of diseases, you should learn about a few of the afflictions that iris may get. Increasingly, horticulturists are sure that if you grow the right plant in the right place and are able to give it the required conditions, the plant will be healthy and vigorous, thus less prone to disease and pests. Today, one of the emphases of iris breeding is disease resistance. In the future, perhaps iris breeders will even look toward genetic engineering to improve their favorite plants.

Unfortunately, environmental conditions are rarely perfect and so irises, though basically resistant to most pathological conditions, occasionally will succumb to diseases. The following are among the more common diseases that irises may get.

BACTERIA

BACTERIAL LEAF SPOT

Bacterial leaf spot (*Xanthomonas tardicrescens*), also called bacterial leaf blight, can affect many irises, including all of the bearded irises and Japanese and Siberian irises. It also can infect *Iris cristata, I. tectorum, I. missouriensis* and *I. tenax*. Not surprisingly, this bacterial disease is easily confused with fungal leaf spot disease. Both occur throughout the United States and both occur most of all during foggy and rainy weather. Irises will get bacterial leaf spot most often during mild weather, while fungal leaf spot can occur anytime the temperature is above freezing.

Bacterial leaf spot causes large irregular spots that first appear near the margins on the leaf tips. At first, the spots are just small pale areas. The key to diagnosing bacterial infections is that the spots appear watery at first, then soon turn light brown. These brown spots become larger and develop whitish or grayish centers. The bacterial infection follows the leaf veins down the leaves and the splotches may run together. Bacterial leaf spot splotches are larger and more irregular than fungal leaf spots.

CONTROL—Since there is no cure, prevention is the only thing that will help control this disease. The bacterium is easily spread on garden tools as well as by water splashing on the plants, so beware of using any tools on healthy plants that have been used on infected plants. Wash your hands thoroughly after working on plants infected by bacterial leaf spot. Disinfect tools with a dilute solution (1 part bleach to 9 parts water) of 0.5 percent sodium hypochlorite (household bleach).

Cultural measures to prevent bacterial leaf spot include removing old foliage from the garden in the fall and destroying it. This will minimize a number of potential iris problems. Since the bacteria do not infect the rhizome, transplanting can be helpful.

BACTERIAL SOFT ROT

Bacterial soft rot (*Erwinia carotovora*) can be a serious problem in bearded irises. It also has been found in Siberian and Japanese irises. The bacteria are common in soils throughout the world. Experts believe that these bacteria are pathogens that get into iris rhizomes and basal plant parts only through injuries—wounds caused by careless gardening practices or by insects. Iris borers are vectors of bacterial soft rot, so try to keep them under control.

You can tell when an iris has bacterial soft rot by the yellow wilting leaves. If you pull gently on the leaves they will come off the plant. There is soft and slimy rot at the base of the plant that has a distinctly foul odor. The foul odor is the clue that tells you this is a bacterial disease. The rhizomes may have holes in them. The bacteria produce a pectolinic enzyme that acts in the plant tissues by digesting the cementing layer of pectin between cells, causing the tissues to lose both form and structure. That is the same pectin found in fruit or added to fruits to make them gel as jams and jellies.

161

Bacterial soft rot is a disease of hot, humid weather and seems particularly prevalent when the temperature is above 80 degrees F and there is lots of moisture at the base of the plant. Heavy soils with low oxygen content and extended periods of rain exacerbate bacterial soft rot problems.

CONTROL—A number of conservative cultural practices will go far in preventing bacterial soft rot infections. If these are followed, it is unlikely that you will have severe problems with this disease.

Irises that are crowded are more prone to bacterial soft rot—this is a very important cultural factor, as good air circulation is very important in keeping irises healthy. Divide and replant irises every three years, especially if they are crowded. Don't grow irises in the shade where they are more likely to be prone to diseases. Let the sun shine on the rhizomes of bearded irises and you will have fewer disease problems.

Be sure that rhizomes are uninjured and dry when planted. Cleaning up and destroying dead iris leaves and the foliage from nearby plants is a good preventive for bacterial soft rot, as well as for iris borers and fungal diseases. Do not compost iris foliage since that might harbor pests and diseases.

Warm, moist conditions encourage soft rot bacteria. Good drainage and good soil structure will help prevent this disease. Handle rhizomes and other roots carefully to avoid injuries by which the bacteria can enter the plants. Raking and weeding are the garden chores most likely to injure irises. Inspect plants often for signs of borers or other insects that can cause injuries through which the bacteria can enter the plants.

Lift any infected rhizomes and cut away all affected tissue. Scrape out all the mushy parts down to solid tissue with a spoon, then place the rhizomes in the sun to dry and callus. Iris growers have discovered that sprinkling the scraped areas with Comet kitchen cleanser, a product containing chlorine bleach, is a good way to get rid of any remaining bacteria or fungi. Letting tall bearded iris rhizomes set in the sun and dry for several days is a good way to treat any that are divided and ready for replanting.

Household bleach (sodium hypochlorite) makes a good antibacterial solution for dipping rhizomes before replanting them. Make a 2 percent drench of ordinary household 5 percent sodium hypochlorite (1 part bleach to 9 parts water) and dip rhizomes; let them dry and then replant.

There seems to be great variation in the susceptibility of different iris varieties. A valuable project for breeders and growers would be to collect data on available varieties and breed for resistance. Listings of resistant varieties would be helpful to all those growing irises.

Bactericides, especially tetracycline, have proven effective in a number of studies on treating bacterial soft rot. For commercial growers, this may have good potential, but for the gardener with a small collection of irises, the previous conservative cultural measures should be more than adequate.

FUNGI

FUNGAL LEAF SPOT

There are many fungal and bacterial organisms that cause leaf spots. *Didymellina macrospora* is a common leaf spot fungus that affects only irises and some of their relatives. It causes small brown spots on the leaves up to $1/4$ inch in size. The spots have reddish borders and may have margins that turn yellow. After the iris blooms, the spots enlarge and may run together to form blotches. Fungal leaf spot, like most fungal diseases, is most prevalent in wet weather.

When the humidity is high and when leaves are wet, the fungal spots produce spores that spread by splashing and by wind to other plants. This fungus spends the winter months on old infected foliage and ground debris.

CONTROL—Clean up, remove and destroy old iris foliage and other ground debris in the late winter before warm weather begins. This will remove many sources of fungal infection as well as other pests and diseases. Do not compost this debris. Grow irises in sunny sites and do not let them get crowded. Place plants far enough apart so that the leaf spot fungus cannot readily spread. Good air circulation is another fungal preventive that works very well. Remove badly spotted foliage and destroy it to prevent further spreading of the leaf spot spores.

FUSARIUM WILT

Fusarium wilt, also known as fusarium basal rot, is caused by the fungus *Fusarium oxysporum* and affects bulbous irises most of all. This fungus causes what is often called "dry rot" of iris bulbs. Symptoms of this disease include stunted yellow leaves. This symptom reflects the fact that the plant has root problems.

The fungus first infects the roots, producing symptomatic brown sunken spots. Then the roots die and the fungus moves on to the bulbs, where gray lesions occur, then turn pale brown or reddish. Fungal infections typically show definite margins between the healthy tissue and the infected spots. As the infection progresses, there may be mats of white or reddish fungus on the bulbs.

Fusarium wilt is most common in warm climates and in sandy soils. This fungal disease is found throughout the world and attacks other bulbous plants as well, including crocus and gladiolus. Oddly, the problem is most serious on the yellow varieties of bulbous irises.

CONTROL—The best way to avoid fusarium wilt is to dig and get rid of diseased plants, replacing them with healthy stock in fresh soil, since this fungus will live for three to four years in the soil. Avoid damaging bulbs and roots when digging irises. When storing bulbs, make sure they are in a well-ventilated place and stored so that each bulb can be dry and have good air circulation around it. Note that acid soils are more hospitable to fusarium wilt than are alkaline soils. Before planting, you can dip the bulbs in a fungicide such as finely ground elemental sulfur or in a dilute solution of household bleach (1 part bleach to 9 parts water).

SCLEROTIUM ROOT ROT

Sclerotium root rot, southern wilt, southern blight, crown rot and mustard seed fungus disease are all names for a serious disease that is caused by a fungus (*Sclerotium rolfsii*) carried in the soil. This disease, a crown rot that can be very serious in spuria irises and bulbous irises, is especially prevalent in the southern states. It is also found on bearded irises and Pacific Coast native irises. Also known as white bulb rot, it is a major fungal disease for spurias. A wide range of plants serve as hosts for this fungus, which grows very fast when it has the right temperatures and moisture. It will thrive on living or dead plant tissue, producing a cottony mass of filaments as it grows.

The first sign of this soilborne fungus probably will be the appearance of slimy rot at the base of the foliage fans and on the growing end of the rhizomes. This rot is caused by an acid emitted by the fungus that kills the living tissue upon which it is growing. Then it grows into the dead tissue. You will also see mycelial webbing of white threads or filaments on the rhizome that will soon cover the entire rhizome. The diagnostic keys are the small round "mustard seeds," fruiting bodies that are tan to brown and appear scattered throughout the mycelium.

Mustard seed fungus thrives in regions noted for mild weather and hot humid summers. Where winter temperatures go to 10 degrees F or below for extended periods of time, it should not be a problem. The exception to this is when the fungus comes in on plants from a warmer climate and does its damage before winter sets in.

If you see only rot and webbing and thus aren't sure which fungus you see, place an affected rhizome complete with rot and mycelium into a plastic bag with a bit of water. Close the bag and look again in a few days. Check for mustard seed fruiting bodies on the mycelium. Note that where there is sclerotium root rot, there also may be secondary infections of bacterial soft rot (Erwinia carotovora) that might confuse the diagnosis. When that occurs, oddly the stink of bacterial rot is not as strong as when it occurs alone—in fact, the odor may be faintly pleasant.

CONTROL—You can prevent fungal diseases, but you can't cure them. Fungicides are preventives and only a few will have any appreciable effect on existing fungal diseases. The most conservative control for sclerotium root rot is to dig and destroy any diseased plants, then replace them with clean plants in new soil. Be sure that the soil drains well and that you do not overwater.

As has been mentioned before, when you buy iris rhizomes, inspect them carefully and, as a preventive measure, dip them in a dilute solution of household bleach (1 part bleach to 9 parts water) and let them dry before planting. This will kill fungal and bacterial organisms as well as insects and other pests.

Perhaps in the near future, some scientifically minded irisarians will choose to study disease resistance in irises. Certainly, a valuable project would be to identify and list irises showing resistance to sclerotium root rot and other diseases. Most gardeners probably would be happy to spend a few cents extra if they knew about the disease resistance of iris cultivars and species.

RUST

Iris rust is caused by the fungus pathogens *Puccinia iridis* and *Puccinia sessilis*. The first, a rusty red fungus, occurs commonly on bearded and bulbous irises and also on the species irises *Iris fulva, I. missouriensis, I. tenax* and

165

I. versicolor. This fungus will spread from leaf to leaf and will overwinter in mild climates. *Puccinia sessilis,* a black rust that appears late in the growing season, also will infect *I. versicolor* and some other plants.

These fungi appear as small oval to oblong spots on leaves and stems that are red to dark brown, or as black powdery spots, depending on which pathogen is infecting the plants. The powdery parts of the spots are the spores that you can easily see with a microscope. The fungal lesions may be surrounded by yellow margins. If there are lots of rust spots, the leaves and stems will die.

Like many fungi, rusts are favored by humid climates and moderate temperatures. Rust is a common and serious problem in the southeastern United States and the foggy coastal areas of the West Coast. Rust is uncommon in the Pacific Northwest. Dew, rain, fog, high humidity and overhead watering all encourage the development of fungi, including rust.

CONTROL—The best way to control rust is to take measures to prevent it. Remove and destroy old foliage in the fall. Don't plant new healthy irises in a spot where you previously have had rust problems. Apparently, there is a lot of variation in different iris varieties' susceptibility to rust.

VIRUSES AND SCORCH
IRIS MOSAIC VIRUS

The worst thing about aphids is that they carry the iris mosaic virus. They are what are called "vectors," the organisms that harbor and transmit the disease. You can easily recognize this viral disease by the streaking or mottling that occurs on the foliage, and also by the stunted growth and distorted flowers that are definitely not up to the quality one expects from irises.

The foliage is mottled or streaked with pale yellow to green areas alternating with the normal green color. Mosaic virus is common throughout the world. Iris mosaic virus is more severe in warm climates and in any places or conditions that favor high aphid populations.

CONTROL—There is no cure or control other than to control the aphids and be aware of what iris mosaic virus symptoms look like. Commercial growers rogue out any plants that begin to show viral signs and destroy them, and you should do the same. You can be sure that commercial growers do everything they can to get rid of any plants that develop mosaic virus. You know you will get healthy, disease-free plants from conscientious growers because they don't want any hint of virus in their plants.

Note that if a garden has some iris varieties that are diseased and you don't remove and destroy them, all the irises will eventually get the disease. But, once the diseased plants are destroyed, you don't have to worry that the virus will be in the garden soil because it can only be vectored by the aphids. This virus is carried in the rhizomes or bulbs and therefore any good control measures call for removing any infected plants as soon as they appear.

SCORCH

Oddly, the cause of scorch in irises is not known, although many horticulturists have studied the problem. Scorch is a pathological condition of bearded irises, but no one knows whether similar conditions in beardless irises are caused by the same pathogen. Scorch is one of the diseases that affects Louisiana irises. Aril and arilbred irises seem to be most susceptible to scorch. It is a condition most common in the southern and central regions of the United States and may occur at any time during the growing season. Discussions about the reasons for scorch are contradictory and confusing. Some say it occurs during wet weather while others believe it comes on more often in dry weather. Various schools of thought associate scorch with nematodes, bacteria and fungi. Others blame pH or the nutrient balances in the soil. No one knows for sure.

Scorch does not appear to be particularly contagious since it will occur only in scattered spots of large plantings. Scorch begins with withering of the central leaves and within a few days the leaves turn a characteristic rusty red-brown, beginning at the tip and spreading down toward the base. Soon all the leaves are affected. At the same time, the roots rot and die, but the rhizome remains firm for a while after the first signs are noticed. The roots become mushy inside, then dry and hollow. Diagnose the plant at this stage by pulling it out of the ground to inspect the rhizome and roots.

CONTROL—Here in Missouri, iris breeder Louise Bellagamba recommends the "Hot Asphalt Treatment" for curing iris scorch. Quite simple, this treatment consists of digging up the affected plants and placing them in a sunny spot on asphalt paving for a week or two and then replanting.

Other iris growers have had good luck if they catch the scorch early and dig the affected plants up, then dry them for about a month until they are ready to grow new roots. If you do this, it may take them two full seasons to bloom once again. In many cases, it will make better sense to discard the diseased plants. For obvious reasons, I wouldn't suggest adding them to the compost heap. Treating the soil with calcium nitrate has helped reduce the occurrence of a similar disease in tulips and gladioli.

A FEW FINAL WORDS

The American Iris Society and its many local and state chapters have members in just about every city and town in the country. The members are generous with information and rich in experience with the many kinds of irises. Search out AIS members in your state when you have iris problems. If one doesn't know the answer, he or she undoubtedly will know of someone who can give you a recommendation for just about any iris problem.

These days, new biological pest and disease controls are coming into the marketplace every year. Try to stay up-to-date on these conservative products and look for local stores where you can find both the products and sources of information on these environmentally sound solutions to pests and diseases.

For chemical recommendations, visit your local garden center. Before you buy pesticides, be sure to read the labels so that you are aware of the dangers and also so that you know exactly what the product will do. Be sure to follow directions carefully, both for the sake of safety and to make sure that the product will do exactly what you want it to do.

Propagating Irises

A seedling bed in the Bennett Jones Garden of Portland, Oregon. (Photograph by Jim Morris.)

Vegetative Propagation
of Irises

There are two main ways to increase the numbers of plants: sexually and asexually. In sexual reproduction, you get a mixing of genetic material with half coming from each of two parents. That is how new cultivars of irises are made. The advantage of sexual reproduction is that breeders can develop new genetic identities that may bring new colors, new flower patterns, greater beauty, increased disease resistance, new forms or other characteristics.

The breeder artificially crosses the two desired parent plants, then grows the seeds, as you will learn in chapter 27. There is also open pollination, also known as open breeding or bee pollination, in which the sexual crosses take place naturally with the help of bees or other insects without any interference from plant breeders.

Asexual propagation of plants includes divisions, cuttings and layerings. Cuttings may be leaves, parts of leaves, stems or roots. Most recently, tissue culture has been added to the palette of plant propagation but, as this is a highly technical laboratory procedure, it is not of concern to most gardeners. Tissue culture involves taking undifferentiated tissue, such as found in root tips, growing tips and plant embryos, and culturing it in special media so that the resulting mass of cells produces tiny new plants. Each new plant is a clone, that is, it is genetically identical to the plant from which the tissue culture was made.

The advantage of asexual propagation is that you can genetically duplicate plants. New iris cultivars are developed through sexual propagation, then they are replicated by asexual reproduction so that many gardeners can enjoy the new creation.

In the case of irises, the main way to increase the number of plants asexually is by division. When you propagate plants by division, you also get clones of the original plant. Again, the important factor is that each of the new plants is exactly the same genetically as its common ancestor. Any differences that may occur in gardens will be due to the care they receive. In order to have consistent plants that all can be called by a certain cultivar name, you must propagate the plants asexually. Thus, the plants of any cultivar all should be clones of one another and have exactly the same genetic makeup.

Recommended planting depths that I am providing are those common for the midwestern United States. These may vary in different parts of the country. For instance, experts recommend planting tall bearded irises 1 or 2 inches deep rather than on the soil surface in parts of Oregon, where there are no iris borers and rhizomes tend not to rot. The nice thing about irises of all types is that their rhizomes, bulbs and roots tend to seek their own optimum depth as long so you plant them at approximately the right depth.

BEARDED IRISES

Rhizomatous bearded irises should be divided every three to five years for them to be most productive. In some regions, growers divide them even more often. After they've been in the ground for more than three years, they may begin to become overcrowded and have fewer flowers. The rhizomes increase and eventually become tangled in a thick mass covering the iris bed. Some kinds are more vigorous and will probably need dividing more often.

Although you can dig and divide bearded irises anytime you can work the ground, the best time for transplanting is when the rhizomes have reached their maximum growth and are semidormant—in July, August and early September in most parts of the United States. The point is to divide the rhizomes and transplant them in time for them to grow new roots during fall months.

If you time things right, you may even have significant blooms from the new divisions next year. If you divide bearded irises in the spring, the plants will probably be fine, but you probably will sacrifice the current year's flowers. If you divide and transplant bearded irises too late in the fall, the plants won't have time to develop new roots and become reanchored in the soil. The result may be that freeze-thaw cycles will heave them out of the ground. Knowing the growing cycles of bearded irises explains the timing of transplanting.

Ensminger iris seedbed, Lincoln, Nebraska. (Photograph by Jim Morris.)

When the soil warms up in the spring, irises begin growing aboveground, developing this year's foliage, buds and flowers. The roots on last year's old rhizomes decay and disappear during this period. At the same time, the new iris roots on this year's productive rhizomes are growing, supplying nutrients and water to the foliage. Once the plants have flowered, rhizome and root growth continue for about two months in this year's blooming rhizomes.

During this stage, nutrients are being stored in the rhizomes for the following season's growth. At this time, the rhizomes develop the new rhizomatous growing ends from which next year's foliage fans and flower buds will arise. The growing productive parts of the rhizomes look like a **Y**. The leg of the **Y** is the older part of the rhizome and the arms are the newer parts where next year's growth will take place.

Once this growing period is over, most of the bearded irises rest until the late-summer rains arrive. The irises are semidormant during these weeks. The exceptions are the reblooming irises that grow continuously throughout the summer and so must constantly gather moisture and nutrients for repeated buds, stalks and flowers. The late-summer rains and slightly cooler weather trigger a new round of root growth. Extra water during hot, dry summer months will cause these irises to begin their late-season period of root growth sooner.

173

The block of time between the period of spring growth and the late-summer period of root growth is optimum for dividing and transplanting bearded irises. During this time, you can work at a leisurely pace on digging the irises, trimming the rhizomes and replanting them, because it will be good for the rhizomes to dry out for a few days. It is best to spread the rhizomes out on newspapers in a dry, shady spot for several days so that they can dry out. Any soft or cut places will develop a corky surface as they dry—this is called callusing.

As an illustration of the tough extremes to which you can put large bearded iris rhizomes, I have left bearded iris rhizome clumps out of the ground lying in the sun for a week or more and they seemed to be better off for it. This is an excellent way to get rid of fungal diseases, especially any root rots that may have crept into the bed. Smaller rhizomes will dry and callus more quickly than large ones. Shorten the drying period for smaller rhizomes.

When digging the iris clumps, make sure you keep them separated correctly according to species or cultivar. Some find it easier to keep the clumps of each variety of bearded iris on separate newspapers together with their labels from the garden bed. Separate the rhizomes and examine them carefully. You may have to cut or break the rhizomes apart. Use a sharp knife to remove soft and diseased parts. Clean the knife after each cut to avoid spreading disease. An easy way to do that is to wipe the blade, then put it into household chlorine solution for a few seconds.

To make it easier to handle and replant them, cut the foliage fans back to a length of 6 to 8 inches from the rhizome. Trim back the smaller bearded irises proportionately. At this point, write the species or variety on the remaining leaves with a dark indelible marker so that identification will not be a problem while you are making new garden labels. Trim up the separate divisions, making sure that each fan of leaves has a short piece of rhizome with healthy, strong feeder roots. Some growers like to make divisions that are **Y**-shaped so that there are two fans per division, each on a smaller arm of the **Y**, and sharing the leg of the **Y**.

When you replant the divisions, make sure that the growing ends of the rhizomes don't face each other. Face them outward so that the plants don't become crowded as fast. When your divisions have been made, trimmed and marked, be sure to let them dry and callus in the sun for a few days. If you do that, you don't need to dip them in fungicide or any other drying or rooting substance.

174

Prepare the new iris beds well, amending the soil with compost, well-rotted cow manure or equivalents. Be sure to prepare the soil to a depth of at least a foot, preferably more if your soil is poor. Although iris rhizomes prefer sitting within view in the top inch of soil, their feeder roots will go much deeper. These irises will tolerate soils that range from sandy loam to heavy clay soils. They also will grow in soils with a pH that ranges from slightly acid to slightly basic.

When replanting the iris divisions, barely cover the upper part of the rhizome with about a half-inch of soil. Smaller rhizomes will need less of a covering. If the rhizomes are left totally uncovered, they may get sunscald. Planting iris rhizomes deeply will encourage fungal diseases, especially root rots. Once the new plants become established, the rhizomes will grow to the level they prefer. Make a planting hole big enough to spread the feeding roots out and downward. Firm the soil around the roots and rhizomes, then water in. The smaller dwarf types of irises can be planted just 5 or 6 inches apart to give a nice immediate effect. The larger intermediate and tall bearded varieties should be planted 1 to 1 1/2 feet apart.

If you want an iris bed that looks established more quickly, you can plant the large rhizomes closer together, but then you will have to divide them sooner. Remember that if you make sure the growing ends of the rhizomes point away from the center of the clump, the irises will not get crowded quite so fast.

Most bearded irises will produce the best bloom in the second, third and fourth years after dividing them. Once they have been in place for five or more years, the centers of the clumps begin to be very crowded and the center rhizomes become less and less productive, with less and less foliage.

SIBERIAN IRISES

Late summer and early fall (late August to September) are the best times for dividing and transplanting Siberian irises. Your chances for success will not be as great if you transplant them right after they bloom or in early spring. Siberian and Japanese irises can be treated similarly in making divisions of their clumps.

Long-established clumps of Siberian irises will be hard to divide because of the snarl of roots they will have developed. Make note of when you divided Siberians and plan to divide them again in another three to four years.

Siberian seedling patch in West Lafayette, Indiana. (Photograph by Jim Morris.)

You may need to pull apart the clumps of slender rhizomes and roots using two garden forks as levers, just as you do with daylilies. Place the forks into the clumps facing away from each other, then pry the handles apart. The resulting leverage should help loosen the Siberian iris root clump.

Each new division should contain about a half dozen of the slim rhizomes. Do not make divisions with fewer than three rhizomes or you will have to wait a longer time to get the typical clumpy look so prized by Siberian iris–lovers. Single rhizomes look very skimpy in garden beds so you would be better off aesthetically to plant several of the same kind together. After digging up the clumps, cut back the foliage to about 4 to 6 inches so that top growth will be minimal while roots grow and are established.

Replant Siberian iris divisions with the rhizomes at a depth of 2 inches and plan to place the divisions 1 to 1 1/2 feet apart. Be sure the planting hole has room for spreading out the long fibrous feeder roots. For the best results, soil for the Siberians should be fertile and moist with a pH on the acid side, about 6.0 or slightly less. Siberian cultivars differ in their tolerance for dry conditions, so you should ask for specific care when you're buying them or at least keep a careful eye on them in your garden. Siberian irises do require good drainage and thrive on even moisture throughout the growing season. If rains don't supply the moisture, be sure to water well whenever soil moisture gets low.

If you buy ready-made divisions through a mail-order nursery, directions may come with the Siberian irises (also Louisiana and Japanese irises) to soak the rhizomes for a day or two to replenish the moisture lost during shipping. If you soak them too long, they will rot. A good clue is to look for a little tip growth as a sign to end the soak. The rate at which the rhizomes begin to rot in the water will depend upon factors such as temperature, light and water quality. Therefore, keep a close eye on soaking rhizomes. In some cases, they will be fine for an extended length of time, but don't count on it. As several iris experts have told me, if you have one very expensive iris, that is the one that will rot or die or have some other unexpected problem.

PACIFIC COAST IRISES

Divisions of Pacific Coast irises should only be made when there is new root growth that has not reached 2 inches or so in length. The season when this occurs will vary depending on the climate, sometimes early spring but more often the fall or winter. For mild climates, the time for PC roots to initiate growth is from late fall through early winter. Check around the base of the plant carefully with your hands or a trowel used gently—look for the fresh white roots that signal that it is time to lift, divide and transplant.

Wash the soil from the roots and divide clumps into separate fans. Trimming back the foliage by one-half will make them easier to handle. Each division should have one or more new roots. Plant the divisions in containers and hold them until new growth appears before putting them in the garden once again. Soil should be highly organic and slightly acid.

Cal-Sibe irises, crosses between some of the Pacific Coast native irises and Siberian irises, can be divided and replanted in spring or early fall. Success will probably be greater if you divide them in late summer to early fall.

LOUISIANA IRISES

These irises should be divided and reset every three years if they are to perform at their maximum. Plan to do this in late summer through mid-fall (August through October) in order for the new divisions to become established before winter cold sets in. These irises grow fast and become crowded quickly. Under good growing conditions, different varieties can grow into each other in a tangled mess of rhizomes faster than you could have imagined. This complicates identification, so beware. Again, using indelible markers to write the cultivar names on the fans will save headaches later if you lose labels.

These are bog plants, so lifting and dividing them from their highly organic, damp soil will be a messy job. Dig up the clump with a garden fork and wash the soil from the roots so they will be easier to separate. Examine the rhizomes carefully, trimming away any dead or diseased areas. Replant divisions, making sure that each fan has good new roots. Replant them at the same depth they were before—since the foliage of Louisiana irises may grow to be 2 to 4 feet tall, there should probably be about 1 to 1 1/2 inches of soil over the rhizomes. Plant so that the growing end of the rhizome is aimed toward the outside of the planting site to lessen crowding. If you leave at least 1 1/2 feet between Louisiana irises, this will defer their invasions of one another's territories. An acid, constantly moist soil that is high in organic matter will suit Louisiana irises.

SPURIA IRISES

Late summer and fall—September in most parts of the country, October in the arid Southwest—is the ideal time for dividing and replanting spuria irises. They are easy to divide, although it may take them up to two years to become established and bloom once again. Moisture-retentive fertile soils will encourage these beardless irises to mature and bloom again. The clumps, which can reach 5 to 6 feet in height, can be left in place for well over a decade if regularly fertilized.

Dig the clump and separate the rhizomes and roots. Examine carefully and remove any dead or diseased parts or rhizomes that are less than vigorous. Trim the foliage to 6 inches or less and mark the variety on a leaf with an indelible marker so you can make a label for it after planting, or note on your garden plan where the new divisions are located. Replant the rhizomes at the same depth they were before in very fertile soil that is neutral to slightly alkaline (a pH of 7.0 or slightly higher). The rhizomes should have about an inch of soil over them.

JAPANESE IRISES

It is necessary to divide these beautiful irises every three years. The best time for dividing and replanting Japanese irises is, like many other kinds of irises, in the late summer to early fall. When you divide the older clumps

Irises add color and variety to many landscape scenes. This is the Pries Garden in St. Louis County, Missouri. (Photograph by Jim Morris.)

during these months, the new divisions will have time to establish and begin growing new roots before winter weather arrives. If you try to divide Japanese iris clumps in the spring, some of the divisions may die and others may fail to bloom during the following season.

Cut back the foliage to about 5 inches to make the plants easier to handle. Dig up an entire clump and use two garden forks as suggested above to pry and lever apart the thick, rhizomatous root mass. From the original clump, separate out some large chunks. New divisions for garden beds should have at lease three fans, although single fans will quickly increase if it is numbers you want. Set the new divisions about 3 inches (deep in rich, highly organic soil that has an acid soil (pH of about 5.5). Never let the rhizomes dry out while dividing and transplanting them.

BULBOUS IRISES

Dig the bulbous irises during their dormant season, anytime after they have bloomed and the foliage has ripened and turned yellow. Separate the small offshoots from the old bulbs and plant them. Discard the old bulbs. Try to avoid nicking and cutting the bulbs as you work with them. Ideally, you should plant these irises 4 inches deep, depending on the species, in sandy loam. Plant larger bulbs about 6 inches deep, a depth of about three times the height of the bulb. They require much the same culture as tulips or daffodils.

179

The use of hybrid irises in this California garden adds variety and charm. (Photograph by Jim Morris.)

HYBRIDIZING IRISES

Growing irises appears to be addictive to some gardeners. Those who prove susceptible to "irisitis" are seldom content for long to grow only other people's cultivars. You can recognize the symptoms of irisitis in gardeners you know when you find them inquiring how to hybridize irises, how to test the offspring and then how to apply for registry of the cultivars they have created. Irises are beautiful and also easy to breed. Those two facts alone are enough to send some people off on an iris-breeding kick.

More iris cultivars are created by dedicated amateurs than by professional gardeners. To be sure, many of these amateurs have gained a depth of knowledge and experience that would match that of most professional horticulturists. If you decide to breed irises, join the American Iris Society and the sections or cooperating societies pertaining to the irises you will work with. This will put you in touch with people who can help you learn because they have been hybridizing irises for many years.

If you are going to breed irises seriously, you must keep good records and label plants properly. The parent plants must be correctly identified and the specific cross must be labeled, both on the parent plant during the period when the seeds are developing and in your own records. A notebook or computer file of records is mandatory for plant breeders. The records should include the full date of the cross and the names of the parent plants, including which is the pollen parent and which is the pod parent. Put the name of the pod parent first, followed by an "x" and then the pollen parent. Include numbered sequences of the crosses you make.

Attach the plant label or tag to the stalk just below the ovary of the pollinated flower.

Choosing irises to breed involves more than just picking two pretty flowers. Knowing the heritage of the cultivars you might consider will provide clues to their potential as a pod or pollen parent. Knowing how well irises have performed in other breeding schedules provides other clues. Analyzing irises you want to cross to see if it might be possible to improve certain weak features shows another road to choosing the parent plants. For instance, you might cross an iris with a beautifully colored flower with one that has better form in the hope that you would get a beautiful flower with improved form. Of course, it might work in reverse and you could have flowers with poorer form and color than either parent.

Those who become extremely involved with breeding irises will learn a lot about chromosome numbers and about what combinations of parents will produce vigorous offspring. The *Iris* genus includes quite a few species that will interbreed successfully, and this potential opens up all kinds of opportunities for the knowledgeable and adventurous iris breeder. Knowing what diploids and tetraploids will cross with what other ones is often a matter of record, and the American Iris Society can help one find the appropriate records or people who know.

The American Iris Society is the international registrar of all irises registered for commerce, with the lone exception of the bulbous irises. The AIS publishes and maintains ten-year summary checklists that are available for purchase. The spring-blooming bulbous irises are registered with the Dutch Bulb Growers Association.

The method of cross-pollinating irises in order to create new cultivars is simple. Rather than having bees or other insects pollinate the flowers, the iris breeder will take the pollen from the selected pollen parent and place it on the stigma of the pod parent. Self-pollination is equally simple, requiring only that pollen be transferred from the stamens of a flower to its own stigma or the stigma of another flower of the same variety. (If you're having trouble identifying the plant parts, see chapter 28, "The Anatomy of Irises.")

When the flower first opens, no pollen is visible because the anthers are closed. Before long, they split open. The pollen grains are ripe and most viable at that time when the pollen appears fluffy. The pod-parent flower is ready to receive the pollen grains when the stigmatic lip has separated from the style branch. At this stage, some three to four hours after the flower opens, the stigma is moist and untouched. To avoid the possibility of the insects beating you to the flowers, plan to make your pollinations early in the morning.

You also can foil the insects by clipping the falls of the pod parent as soon as possible. Then the bees will have no landing platform. Removing the stamens, the filaments with their anthers, before or just at the time of the natural opening of the bloom also thwarts the insects. To be absolutely sure there is no opportunity for insects to pollinate the flowers, some plant breeders either cage the plants in insect-proof covers or bag the flowers with insect-proof, tightly woven cloth. After pollinating the female parent, they bag that flower again. Bagging the flower after fertilization also prevents invasion by the verbena bud moths that can invade and severely injure seedpods. A further protection is to stake the stalk to help protect it from dogs, children and other potential hazards.

To collect from the pollen parent, the hybridizer clips the anthers from the stamens of the desired pollen parent and dabs them onto all three stigmas of the chosen pod parent if there is plenty of pollen on the anthers. The pollen grains will stick to the stigma surfaces. Tweezers are handy for this job and a small cup or plastic container is handy for holding the anthers. Place the anthers of each pollen parent in a separate container and put the anthers in the container with the pollen-side up.

If you are collecting pollen-laden anthers from several iris flowers, be sure to thoroughly wash and wipe the tweezers between flowers, and carefully mark each container with the variety name. If the pollen grains do not seem plentiful, you can pollinate only one or two of the pod parent's stigmas. When you pick the anthers, include parts of their filaments to use as handles.

If you only want to see if you are capable of pollinating the flowers, simply use a soft watercolor brush and dab your way through the garden. Dab the brush on the stamens of one iris flower to pick up the ripe pollen grains, then dab the brush on the stigmatic lip of another flower. Undoubtedly, this will create some interesting crosses. Without a record of the parentage and without making sure that insect pollination does not take place, you can't be sure of the parentage and so won't be able to register any outstanding specimen you might create, except with the caveat "parentage unknown."

Each viable pollen grain that lands on a stigma will develop a slender tube that grows down from the stigma through the style of the pistil, into the ovary and, finally, into an ovule, an embryonic seed containing the egg cell. Each pollen grain contains two sperm nuclei. These nuclei travel down the pollen tube and are released into the ovule, where one nucleus unites with another to form the zygote that will then become the embryonic plant. The second nucleus from the male parent unites with one or two other nuclei to form the cell mass called the endosperm. The endosperm is the part that provides nutrients to the developing embryonic seed. Each viable iris seed is the result of one or more pollen grains placed on the stigma. This double-barreled fertilization of the plant embryo and of the endosperm is part of the development of every iris seed.

Sometimes the blooming times of irises are not compatible for cross-pollination. When that occurs, choose the earlier-blooming iris as the pollen parent and store the pollen in the refrigerator until the pod parent comes into bloom. A temperature of between 35 and 38 degrees F will keep iris pollen viable for about six weeks. Store the pollen in small envelopes or similar containers. Film-cartridge cases or the small plastic containers that fishing flies come in are suitable.

When irises are too distantly related, it may not be possible to successfully cross-pollinate them. Sometimes when the pod and pollen parents are too closely related, they will not successfully cross-pollinate. Some plants are self-sterile, also called self-incompatible, and these must be outcrossed to other varieties. This is also true in other well-known plants. Many apple trees, for instance, need to have their flowers pollinated by other cultivars in order to form fruit.

Sometimes, the breeding parts of the parent plants are incompatible, as is the case when the pollen tubule is incompatible with the tissue of the style, the neck of the pistil. Other reasons for failure in pollination are that the pollen might not be fully ripe or that the stigma is not ripe enough and therefore not ready to receive the pollen. Unfavorable weather conditions can also frustrate attempts to cross-pollinate irises.

In the future, when genetic manipulation has progressed even further than it already has, it may be possible to combine—a better word than "cross" in this case—two distantly related irises through recombinant gene techniques. This means taking desirable genes, the building blocks of chromosomes, from one plant and putting them into another. Recombinant genetics is space-age breeding, using complex techniques. Although the majority of amateur breeders, even skilled ones, probably will never perform these delicate tasks, it doesn't hurt to know what's coming in the future.

This combination of gametes (sperms and eggs) to form the precursors of new organisms (zygotes) is the key to the advantages of sexual crosses that represent a mixing of genetic materials. Every living organism has a number of chromosomes that remains constant throughout its life. Each gamete of a given organism contains just half the number of the organism's regular chromosome number. That is called the haploid number. When two gametes join to form a zygote, the early-stage embryo that becomes a new individual, this offspring has a new combination of chromosomes that represents both parents. Half of the gene-bearing chromosomes come from the female parent and half from the male parent.

Once fertilizations are successful, the ovary area will begin to swell and form the seedpod. This will become obvious in about seven to ten days. The entire process from pollination to ripe seedpod will take between sixty and eighty days. The walls of the ovule harden to protect the enclosed embryo. The ovule, with its hard walls, is now called a seed. The seedpod matures, remaining firmly on the stalk, and slowly turns from green to tan to brown. The seeds are ripe when the seedpod begins to crack at the top, splitting the triangular sections and showing the seeds within.

Preserve and save all of the seeds by removing the pod from the stalk when it begins to crack and placing it in a small paper bag. One pod may produce up to seventy-five seeds. Keep the bag in a cool, dry place and let the seeds continue ripening until they are dry and hard. One should shell out the seeds and allow them to dry. If they are left in the pod they may mold. The exception to this is in the case of spuria iris seeds, which should be sown before they dry out. Separate the seeds from the pods and pieces of pod, then examine them carefully. Cull any that are smaller or deformed, as they may represent incomplete fertilizations that lack either the endosperm or embryo.

Iris seeds are durable. In nature, they fall from the plant and soon are covered by plant detritus. Some seeds may germinate in the fall. In the spring, other seeds will begin to grow, while others may not. Germination of a particular crop of seeds in garden beds may stretch out over fifteen or more years, thus guaranteeing the survival of the offspring as a group. If stored at temperatures that are a bit above freezing, most iris seeds will remain viable for many years. Thus, irises have what are termed macrobiotic seeds capable of surviving more than fifteen years. On the other hand, some iris seeds are notoriously difficult to germinate, including those of *Regelia* and *Oncocyclus* irises, according to iris experts.

The iris seeds have built-in germination inhibitors that slow or prevent growth until conditions are right. The triggers for germination of iris seeds include a required period of dormancy, temperature, oxygen and moisture. In addition, the seed coat may be very hard and keep water and air from reaching the embryonic seed. Mechanically notching a hole in the seed coat will encourage germination by allowing moisture and air to reach the embryo. Soaking the seeds in water before planting also may wash away inhibitors and soften the seed coat enough to allow germination.

Most iris seeds are best planted in the fall. In areas where winter months are very cold, do not plant too early in the fall because then they might sprout before winter. Tender seedlings might freeze if not well protected from severe weather. When planted in October in USDA Zones 5 and 6, there usually is time enough for the seeds to dry out, but it is too late for them to germinate in the fall. The seeds will be ready to grow when warm weather returns.

Some growers plant their iris seeds in cold frames with loose, friable soil that has been amended with plenty of rich loam and well-rotted compost. Others plant iris seeds in hotbeds heated with electric cables, or with heat from rotting manure in the old-fashioned way. Still others plant the seeds in slightly raised beds in the open garden. For the required pH and other requirements for different kinds of irises, check under the "Culture" sections for the various irises in earlier chapters.

Plant the seeds close together, about a seed diameter apart, 1 inch deep in rows that are about 4 inches apart. Mark each row with a label that includes the names of the parent plant and the number of the cross—the same information that was on the seed stalk of the pod parent. Each step of the development from seed to mature plant should be accompanied by these information labels. Also record the dates of planting and various transplantings in the notebook dedicated to your irises. Cover the seeds and lightly tamp the soil.

Once the seeds are planted, some growers like to apply a loose mulch of hay or leaves a couple of inches thick. Water the seedbed well and then keep the soil moist but not wet. Old screens placed on cold frames will protect the seedbed from animals and also cut raindrops into a finer size. To get a head start on spring growth, remove the screens and the hay mulch in January and put framed glass or plastic covers over the cold frames. Be sure to ventilate on hot, sunny days.

In Zones 5 and 6, seed growth will begin in late March in protected cold frames, or in late April where the seedbeds are in the open. The mulch can remain on open seedbeds throughout the winter months. By mid-May, remove cold-frame covers and mulches from open beds, but be prepared to re-cover for cold snaps, torrential rains or hail.

Don't expect all the seeds to germinate. In fact, many iris seeds will germinate the second year, so watch the planting sites for this pattern. As described above, a lot depends on the particular crosses that were made and also on both climatic conditions and your garden techniques. Once the seedlings are 1 to 2 inches tall, transplant them to rows in a well-drained sunny location. Tall bearded irises should be about a foot apart, miniature dwarf bearded irises about 1 to 6 inches apart, and those in between at relative distances apart. At this stage, the rhizomes have appeared but are still very small. While transplanting the small seedlings, be sure not to let the roots dry out.

Begin a weekly schedule of fertilizing with a weak mix of water-soluble fertilizer formulated for flowering plants. This will keep the seedlings growing vigorously. If the young irises grow rapidly throughout the growing season, some may bloom the following year. Once the young irises bloom, you will quickly know if there are any to keep and propagate. Following the bloom period, move any desirable plants wherever you want them for either ornamentation or further growth and eventual propagation.

If any seedlings appear to be less vigorous, off in foliage color or otherwise not pleasing, rogue them out. Always grow seedlings for two years, then evaluate and rogue out. Since you may have dozens of plants from a single cross, you will want to weed out any that don't meet ideals, from the seedling stage to the flowering finale. If there are six or eight really fine irises from a single crossbreeding, you are very fortunate. If a truly fine iris appears, it will have to be reproduced vegetatively from that moment on, because the possible genetic combinations are so vast that you might never get the same exact genetic results from a cross between the same two parent plants.

Judge iris flowers from crossbreedings harshly. There are thousands of named irises already in the marketplace. Judge first for flower color, then for flower form; then examine the plant as a whole to see if the flower is in good proportion. See if the stalk and branching meet the ideals set by the American Iris Society. Study the whole iris plant to see if the overall appearance of the plant is especially pleasing. Any plant that falls down on one or more counts should be rogued out. However, rogue losers only after the second bloom season, as the first-year seedlings are impossible to evaluate.

Those who are serious about breeding irises should definitely join the American Iris Society. AIS chapters exist throughout the country and their members are friendly, generous with their knowledge and good sources of information. Judging seminars exist that prepare members for judging iris shows and irises in the garden. These are the two separate categories for judging. Judging seminars are extremely valuable in teaching people what to look for in the various kinds of irises. I can't imagine anything that would be more helpful to those who want to breed irises.

Lest you think that there are no more challenges in the field of breeding irises, I offer a quote from iris breeder Dave Niswonger of Cape Girardeau, Missouri, who recently wrote in his catalog:

> I marked (for further evaluation) two of the tetraploid Cal-Sibes coming from seed sent to me by Tomas Tamberg of Berlin, Germany. Dr. Tamberg has really made great strides in crossing some of the species that are not very closely related. In this case he took 40-chromosome Siberian irises and crossed them with the 40-chromosome Pacific Coast native irises and then when the seeds were germinating, he treated them with a substance to double the chromosomes (colchicine is often used) and ended with 80-chromosome plants. They have been crossed with each other for further advancements. There are so many avenues of hybridizing that it is truly mind boggling.

The Botany of Irises

Chapter 28

THE ANATOMY OF IRISES

If science is not your strong suit, or if you are a reasonably recent convert to the art and craft of growing irises, the next two chapters may not be particularly exciting. Once our basic needs are met, however, we human beings seem to put a lot of effort into sorting things out, and these two chapters can put irises into convenient pigeonholes. That is what these two chapters are all about. First of all, the anatomy and structure of irises are the subject for discussion.

The points made in this chapter are based upon the physical characteristics of iris plants. These are the factors upon which the botanical classification of plants relies, and that is the subject of the following chapter. As I said, if science is not your favorite subject, skip these chapters, but remember that they are here if your curiosity leads you into finding out more about the many beautiful members of the genus *Iris*.

What do you see when you look at irises in bloom? What kinds of plants are they? First of all, the foliage is grasslike with the same sort of parallel veining you find in grasses, lilies and orchids. Next, you notice that the swordlike leaves don't seem to have stems, but usually rise from ground level. In actuality, the rhizomes, bulbs and corms of irises are modified stems, as we shall see.

The tripartite look of the flower, with three standards and three falls, is a singular characteristic of irises, lending grace and beauty in combination with spectacular colors that are hard to beat. These botanically significant traits will help you better understand irises. I think that knowing something about the botany of irises deepens the enjoyment you get from them.

Irises are angiosperms, the scientific term for flowering plants. There are some 250,000 flowering plants in the world, according to current thought. The parallel veining in the leaves and flower parts that are in multiples of three are clear signs that irises are monocotyledons. The word "monocotyledon" means that these plants have single seed leaves, the third significant clue for monocots. Another important characteristic of monocotyledons is that the vascular bundles—the circulatory systems of plants—are distributed throughout the plant tissue, unlike the ring arrangement of vascular bundles in dicotyledons. Lilies (*Lilium* spp.) and daylilies (*Hemerocallis* spp.) also are well-known monocots of the ornamental-garden world. Monocotyledons as a group are divided into those that have petaled flowers like the irises and those that don't, like the plants of the Gramineae or grass family.

Within these vascular bundles are the tissues that carry water and nutrients up from the roots to the green foliage. This tissue is called the xylem. The phloem is the vascular tissue that carries carbohydrates, the products of photosynthesis, down from the foliage to the roots, rhizomes and bulbs. Green plants are the only organisms that can manufacture nutrients, using sunlight, water and carbon dioxide to produce simple carbohydrates. That is why green plants are placed at the bottom of the food chain. All other life, plant and animal alike, can trace its survival back to green plants used as foods.

Angiosperms fall into two groups, the monocotyledons described above and dicotyledons, the term for those plants having two seed leaves. Unlike monocots with their three-part flowers, the flower parts of dicots develop in fours or fives or multiples of fours and fives. Dicotyledon plants have netlike leaf veining and vascular bundles that are arranged in rings. This group is well represented in the garden by the flowering shrubs, fruit trees, roses, zinnias and many others. But, back to the monocotyledons, where the irises are a significant genus in this plant group.

The three-part flowers of irises form singly or severally on branches of the flower stalks. Each iris flower has three uprights (standards) and three falls, the later, more correctly, the sepals. They usually lie flat or turn down toward the stem. One or more flower buds are enclosed within two modified leaves that are often called spathes. The spathes may be papery or thicker in texture.

The spathes vary in color, texture, shape and size from species to species. Therefore, they can be important in the identification of irises. They can

191

also be of value in trying to guess the heritage of unknown irises, since spathe characteristics may be among the more obvious distinctions that are carried through from ancestral plant parents.

Iris flowers differ widely in appearance and in size, as well as in the relative sizes of their parts. Not only do they come in a dazzling array of colors, color combinations and color patterns, but they also, from species to species throughout the genus *Iris*, have an overall iris look while exhibiting many variations on the theme.

The major flower parts include the standards (petals), falls (sepals), perianth tube, stamens (male organs) and the pistils (female organs), including stigma, style and ovary. The standards and falls have come up for discussion so many times in this book that they probably don't need any further identification or explanation other than to say that these are the plant parts upon which iris breeders concentrate. The characteristics of species and cultivars are reflected most positively through the colors and color patterns of the standards and falls. Together, the standards and falls make up what is collectively called the perianth.

The stamens are the pollen-bearing male organs of the iris flower. They are made up of the anthers at the top, which bear the pollen grains, and the filaments that are the stems of the stamens. In the iris flower, the stamens are located under the style and facing the claw of the branches.

In the iris flowers, the ovary is inferior, that is, it lies at the bottom of the flower. The perianth tube surrounds the pistils and connects the ovaries with the perianth. The ovary is the ovule-bearing structure that is at the base of the flower. Fertilization of the ovules occurs when the tubes of the pollen grains grow through the style into the ovary. The style connects the ovary with the style, which is positioned opposite the falls. The style branches have two little "wings" called crests that shelter the stigma. The stigma is the ridge or lip located at the top of the undersurface of the style branch, and it is here that pollen grains must be deposited to begin the process of pollination.

Iris flowers, like the flowers of other plants, have evolved over millions of years with a single purpose: to develop seeds and thus ensure the future of the parent plant. The form, color and often the aroma combine to attract insects and thus increase the chances of pollination and subsequent development of seeds. In the case of irises, the beard or crest, the signal and the structure of the falls attract insects and provide the pollinators with a landing platform. When the insects reach forward and into the nectar-bearing tube of the flowers, they brush by the pollen-carrying anther, picking up pollen grains. Visiting another flower to take more nectar, they brush by the wet stigma to which the pollen grains adhere. Today's powerful microscopes help botanists study pollen grains, the apertures of which vary in important ways and often are part of the basis for iris classification.

While the foliage of all of the irises is usually sword-shaped with parallel veining, there is a great deal of variety in the many species. Iris leaves often have a waxy coating or bloom that is grayish in color. The texture of the leaves varies from species to species, from thick to thin, from rigid to pliable and from soft to hard. The fans of leaves are vertical and each leaf blade usually is broader at the base.

Folds on the inward edges of the leaves act as sheaths to hold the leaves tightly together, with the base of each leaf nesting inside the leaf behind it. While the flat, sword-shaped leaf is the most common type in the *Iris* genus, some species have leaves that are nearly cylindrical or square or channeled in cross section. If the leaves are channeled, the underside may have a pronounced keel.

Irises can be divided into two main groups according to the types of underground structures they have. The first group has fibrous roots plus modified stems called rhizomes that usually grow horizontally at or near the soil surface. This group includes all of the bearded irises plus the beardless Siberian, Pacific Coast, Louisiana, spuria and Japanese irises.

The second group of irises has fibrous roots plus bulbs, another type of modified stem that consists of fleshy scale leaves that surround a bud plus a short stem. Included within this group are the reticulated, *Xiphium* (often called Dutch, Spanish or English irises) and scorpio or juno irises. Juno irises are bulbous and also have thick, fleshy storage roots, these being the characteristic that distinguishes them from the *Xiphium* irises.

There is one species that falls between the two main groups, being neither rhizomatous nor bulbous. That is *Iris nepalensis,* which is, as you might guess from the species name, native to the temperate regions of the Himalayan Mountains, including the country of Nepal. Both rhizomes and bulbs are rootlike storage structures that make it possible for plants to buffer vagaries of climate.

Both rhizomes and bulbs store nutrients and moisture, then give them up to the rest of the plant when needed. The bulbs have differing coats (tunics), depending upon the iris group they are in. Bulb coatings may be reticulated (netted), papery or thick and leathery. The fibrous roots may be plentiful or scanty depending upon the iris type. They may be thick like those of tall bearded irises or thin and even wiry like those of spuria irises. Some irises, including the evansia irises of damp woodlands, are able to spread by means of slender horizontal stems called stolons that grow out from the main plant near the soil surface.

The rhizomatous irises can be further divided according to the type of feature they have along the center of their falls. The bearded or pogon irises all have a distinctive pattern of long hairs along the top of the basal half of the falls called the beard. Other irises have crests and still others have merely a smooth ridge. Often there are signals on the falls, patches of color that contrast with the rest of the falls. The signals serve as guides to help orient pollinating insects, directing them toward the nectar source along a path where their bodies will brush against the anthers and stigmas.

The seedpods or capsules are based on three parts, just as are the flowers, and they differ greatly in specific size and shape. Botanists make use of seeds, seedpods and flowers in classifying irises, especially the beardless species. Some seedpods are short while others are long. Some are stocky while others are slim. Some are quite round while others show their three sections distinctly. Some iris seedpods are strongly ribbed. Iris seeds may be rough or smooth. Some iris seeds have loose, shiny coatings. The seeds of aril irises, including *Oncocycluses, Regelias* and *Hexapogons,* have fleshy, creamy-white appendages at one end. These arils are important features for the classification of these iris groups. The seeds of Louisiana irises are corklike and float.

THE CLASSIFICATION
OF IRISES

Since before recorded time, humans have spent a lot of time and effort trying to sort out plants and their relationships. The science devoted to this sorting out or classification is known as taxonomy or systematics. One might think that at this point in time all of the classification has been accomplished, but that is hardly the case. Scientists and knowledgeable laypeople argue the fine points of taxonomy and heated discussions can take place over the concept of species. I have seen and heard a few of these arguments and can attest to the fact that both sides often make their points clearly and convincingly—and often, loudly.

Generally speaking, plant taxonomists can themselves be classified into two main groups: lumpers and splitters. The lumpers are inclined to classify plants into larger groups, joining smaller groups into larger ones. Splitters, on the other hand, will form new species and new genera, taking plants out of larger groups and making new subgroups based on slight physical differences. The arguments are fiery when lumpers and splitters meet.

What is the value of botanical taxonomy, the classification of plants, to gardeners? The scientific name includes two, usually Latin, names that represent first, the genus name and, second, the species name of the plant. Knowing this binomial scientific name of a plant will make it possible to clearly identify that particular plant anywhere in the world because the scientists of the botanical world recognize this system, no matter what the country, territory or language.

That is not the case with common names. Too often, gardeners search for plants by their common names and get the wrong plant as a result. Some common names—forget-me-not and bluebell, for example—are used with more than one plant species. When you choose plants from a catalog or at a favorite local nursery, have a resource handy that will provide both the common name(s) and the scientific name. The scientific name provides the precise and worldwide identification for any plant.

Systematics or taxonomy also provides precise information on the relationships among plants or animals. Knowing plant relationships often helps in suggesting what the culture of a plant should be, as plants with similar genetic makeups often require much the same environmental conditions and also are grouped together in the various botanical divisions. Plant origins, histories, discoverers or their friends, and physical descriptions are sometimes implicit in the botanical names of plants.

Iris mandschurica, for instance, is an iris that originally grew in Manchuria and parts of eastern Russia. You might guess this from the Latinized species name. *I. germanica* refers to a number of plants with a long history in central Europe, some of which are described in chapter 1. The species name of *I. reichenbachii* is the Latinized version of Reichenbach. This iris was named in honor of the German botanists Heinrich G. L. Reichenbach and Heinrich G. Reichenbach, father and son, German botanists of the eighteenth and nineteenth centuries, by Johann Heuffel (1800–1857), a Hungarian botanist. *I. pallida* has as a species name the Latin word for "pale," which refers to the silvery appearance of the bracts of this plant.

Irises, from the small, shade-loving, crested irises to the tall bearded irises of sunny sites, all belong to the genus *Iris*. There are some two hundred species of iris native to the North Temperate Zones of the world, most of which bloom regularly in the spring or early summer, and sometimes again later in the season. In addition, there are thousands of named varieties that have been bred or selected for their desired attributes to make them better in some ways for garden use. These often are called cultivars, which simply means "cultivated varieties."

To develop these named varieties or cultivars, professional and amateur plant breeders have selectively bred species to species, species to cultivars, cultivars to cultivars and, indeed, any cross between irises that results in viable seeds. As the science and technology of recombinant genetics develop, there may be some surprising iris crosses down the road that formerly were not possible because of previously incompatible genotypes. In an age when you can take apart and recombine the genetic makeup of highly diverse plants and animals, who knows what lies ahead?

When the science of botanical classification, taxonomy, was first established in the 1700s by Carolus Linnaeus, the basis for classification was the gross anatomy of the flowers and seeds, the sexual parts of the plants. The name of the Swedish botanist and naturalist is usually spelled in the Latin way because he wrote his definitive books in the Latin language. It was *Species Plantarum,* published in 1753, that was the basis for the classification of plants.

In recent years, the bases for classification have expanded to include cellular structure as well as genetic structure. Chromosome numbers and other features of the hereditary factors have become important to taxonomists. Chromosome numbers are also important to iris breeders who often hope to increase the chromosome numbers of new irises through the use of certain chemicals. One of the most successful substances used to increase the chromosomal number is colchicine, a derivative of a *Colchicum* (crocus) species.

As already described, irises all fall within the genus *Iris*. The way I learned it years ago, the classification hierarchy goes as follows: kingdom, phylum, class, order, family, genus, species, variety. Over the years, this descending order to species has remained essentially the same, with the only major changes being the addition of subgroup, as in subgenus, sections and series between genus and species.

The larger groups are split into smaller groups, each successive group being defined by particular structures, especially the structures of flowers and the physiognomy of seeds. First of all, irises fall within the plant kingdom. The next division, or phylum, is the Spermatophyta, or seed plants. This group or subphylum includes Gymnospermae, the cone-bearing plants, and Angiospermae, the flowering plants.

Within the groups of angiosperms, as has already been defined, are the plants belonging to the class called Monocotyledonae, those with single seed leaves, and the plants belonging to the class known as Dicotyledonae, those herbaceous and woody plants with two seed leaves. The monocots are further divided into those with petaloid flowers, those with petals and sepals (such as the irises) and those such as grasses and sedges that have no perianth.

The classes and subclasses are further divided into relatively large plant groups called orders, and then divided once again into groups called families. The irises fall within the plant family known as Iridaceae, the group identified by its tripartite pattern of stamens, petals and an inferior ovary. The plant family is really the botanical group that you should be most familiar with.

The iris family, Iridaceae, consists of about eighty genera and 1,700 species native to temperate and tropical regions around the world. In addition to the true irises, the family includes gladioli, freesias and crocuses, all of which have root structures called corms. The family is distinguished by herbaceous plants with showy bisexual flowers issuing from a spathe of two or more herbaceous, leaflike bracts.

In recent times, scientists have been able to identify DNA sequences of chromosomes. The data from these studies are valuable in determining the relationships among irises. This kind of cellular data is what calls the shots in contemporary taxonomy. Chromosomal cytology, the science of genetic materials, has uncovered iris relationships that were obscured by differing aspects of the gross anatomy of the plants.

Although many people may assume that all of the world's iris species have already been collected and identified, that just isn't so. Plant collecting in regions that are likely to have iris species growing wild is unfortunately complicated by wars, challenging geography, natural hazards such as snakes and other dangerous conditions. Thus opportunities to collect new iris species remain and, if iris species previously unknown are identified, classified and used in iris breeding, our world of horticulture will be far richer as a result.

Sometimes known species of irises are threatened by other circumstances. For instance, there is a central Asian iris (*Iris winkleri*) that may be in danger of extermination because it is being heavily harvested from the wild to sell in cities and no one propagates the species. Crossing that iris with Siberian irises might result in better irises for far northern climates.

According to Brian Mathew, an expert on the genus *Iris*, there are some 250 species of the *Iris* genus, all occurring in north temperate regions. The species are divided into a number of quite distinct groups. Whether we call them subgenera, sections, series or even separate genera, these groupings often have horticultural implications as well as taxonomic and geographical cohesion. Mathew classifies irises in the following way:

GENUS *IRIS*

1. *Iris* subgenus Iris (bearded irises).
   - A. Section *Iris* (bearded or pogon irises), see chapters 8–12.
   - B. Section *Psammiris* (aril irises, rare in trade).
   - C. Section *Oncocyclus* (aril irises), see chapter 13.
   - D. Section *Regelia* (aril irises), see chapter 13.
   - E. Section *Hexapogon* (aril irises, extremely rare).
   - F. Section *Pseudoregelia* (aril irises, rare in trade).
2. Iris subgenus *Limniris* (beardless rhizomatous irises).
   - A. Section *Lophiris* (evansia irises).
   - B. Section *Limniris*.
      - (a) Series *Chinenses* (extremely rare in trade).
      - (b) Series *Vernae* (North American woodland native).
      - (c) Series *Ruthenicae* (rare in trade).
      - (d) Series *Tripetalae* (unusual in trade).
      - (e) Series *Siberica* (Siberian irises), see chapter 14.
      - (f) Series *Californicae* (Pacific Coast irises), see chapter 15.
      - (g) Series *Longipetalae* (Rocky Mountain irises).
      - (h) Series *Laevigatae* (includes Japanese irises), see chapter 18.
      - (i) Series *Hexagonae* (Louisiana irises), see chapter 16.
      - (j) Series *Prismaticae* (North American native iris).
      - (k) Series *Spuriae* (spuria irises), see chapter 17.
      - (l) Series *Foetidissimae* (roast beef plant or Gladwyn iris).
      - (m) Series *Tenuifoliae* (Asiatic irises rare in trade).
      - (n) Series *Ensatae* (the correct name for the Japanese grown as *Iris koempferi*).
      - (o) Series *Syriacae* (Asiatic irises rare in trade).
      - (p) Series *Unguiculares* (winter-flowering dwarf iris).
3. Iris subgenus *Nepalensis* (obscure Asian irises not presently in the trade).
4. Iris subgenus *Xiphium* (English, Dutch and Spanish irises), see chapter 20.
5. Iris subgenus *Scorpiris* (juno irises), see chapter 21.
6. Iris subgenus *Hermodactyloides* (reticulated irises), see chapter 22.

Below the classification groups shown above are species and varieties. The value of the above chart for most gardeners is to show the relationships of the several horticultural iris groupings to the botanical groups. Learning all of the many botanical terms is hardly necessary for most iris growers. This chart undoubtedly will be handy in understanding the relationships of our garden irises and helpful if you should get an unusual iris that is not often in the marketplace.

Again, as noted earlier in the book, the Species Iris Group of North America, a section of the American Iris Society, is the best place to learn more about unusual species and where to find them. Mathew's book *The Iris* also is a rich resource for learning about not only the classification of irises but also where irises are native to, and what ones are likely to be grown successfully.

As you can see, there are many more irises than are described in this book or grown in American gardens. In the future, it is highly likely that new irises will be introduced into our horticultural worlds via catalogs and plant nurseries. In the meantime, take a good look at some of the beautiful new cultivars that iris breeders have introduced recently. New colors, combinations and patterns are available in a variety of sizes. Match the irises to your garden conditions and you will have plants that are as vigorous as they are beautiful.

Below you will find the various iris societies listed with their membership chairperson, including the parent organization, usually the American Iris Society. Most of the specific iris societies listed are officially part of the American Iris Society. The societies for aril irises and Louisiana irises are independent organizations that have affiliations with AIS. In addition to these iris groups, there are many regional and local chapters. The American Iris Society can put you in touch with one or more iris societies in your area.

American Iris Society, Marilyn Harlow, P.O. Box 55, Freedom, CA 95019-0055

Aril Society International (an AIS cooperating society), Audrey Roe, 2816 Charleston NE, Albuquerque, NM 87110

Dwarf Iris Society, Lynda Miller, 3167 E. U.S. 224, Ossian, IN 46777

Historic Iris Preservation Society, Ada Godfrey, 9 Bradford Street, Foxborough, MA 01035

Median Iris Society, Suzanne Sluizer, 3600 Calle del Ranchero NE, Albuquerque, NM 87110

Reblooming Iris Society, Charlie Brown, 3114 S. FM 131, Denison, TX 75020

Society for Japanese Irises, Carol Warner, 16815 Falls Road, Upperco, MD 21155

Society for Louisiana Irises (an AIS cooperating society) Elaine Bourque, 1812 Broussard Road E, Lafayette, LA 70508

Society for Pacific Coast Native Irises, Adele Lawyer, 4333 Oak Hill Road, Oakland, CA 94605

Society for Siberian Irises, Howard Brookins, N 75 W 14257 North Point Drive, Menomonee Falls, WI 53051-4325

Species Iris Group of North America, Colin Rigby, 18341 Paulson SW, Rochester, WA 98579

Spuria Iris Society, Bobbie Shepard, 3342 W. Orangewood, Phoenix, AZ 85051

GLOSSARY

AB. Arilbred iris.

AIS. American Iris Society.

Amoena. The term for a bearded iris flower with white standards and colored falls.

Anther. The part of the stamen of a seed-bearing plant that bears the pollen.

Anthocyanin. The most common cell or sap fluid in irises, producing blue to violet to purple colors.

Apogon. The term for rhizomatous irises that have neither beards nor crests.

AR. Aril iris.

Aril. The white collar surrounding the hilum, point of attachment to the seedpod, on seeds of *Regelia, Pseudoregelias* and *Oncocyclus* irises. These irises also are known as arils.

ASI. Aril Society International.

BB. Border bearded iris with flower stalks that grow 16 to 27 inches tall (see chapter 9 on median irises).

Bicolor. An iris flower with falls and standards of two different colors.

Blend. An iris flower with both blue or purple and yellow or pink pigments.

Chlorosis. Loss of or reduced development of chlorophyll, the green pigment in plants that is responsible for photosynthesis. This is due to some environmental deficiencies or gluts.

Chromosome. One of several to many parts of the cell nucleus that includes genes in linear helical forms. The numbers of chromosomes are commonly constant for any given species or variety.

Clone. A plant that has been reproduced vegetatively and thus has the same genetic makeup as its parent plant.

Crest. The ridge that occurs on the restricted part of the falls of evansia iris flowers.

Cultivar. A cultivated variety, often a clone, that is important in horticulture and is either selected or hybridized. Cultivars should be distinguished from botanical varieties, which are subdivisions of species.

Cytogenetics. The scientific study of cellular components and mechanisms of heredity, including both chromosomes and other cellular components.

Diploid. An organism that has two sets of chromosomes, one set usually from each parent.

DNA. Deoxyribonucleic acid, the cell substance that carries genetic information.

Endosperm. The plant tissue that surrounds the embryo and contains stored nutrients to feed the embryonic plant.

Eupogon. The noun or adjective used to refer to true bearded irises.

Filament. The stamen stalk.

Gamete. A mature germ cell, the male or female germ cell of a sexually reproducing plant or animal.

Genus. The taxonomic group that comes between family and species, and includes a number of species with common characteristics.

Haft. The constricted portion or "neck" of the standards and falls of iris flowers.

Halo. An iris flower with falls and sometimes standards outlined with a band of a lighter or different color.

Haploid. A noun or adjective referring to half the usual number of chromosomes. Diploid germ cells have haploid numbers of chromosomes.

Heterosis. Another term for hybrid vigor, the superiority of a hybrid over either of its parents in any of several qualities.

Hexaploid. Having six sets of chromosomes.

Hilium. The scar that marks the point of attachment of a seed to its seedpod.

HIPS. Historic Iris Preservation Society.

Hybrid. An organism resulting from the breeding of two genetically dissimilar parents.

IB. Intermediate bearded iris with plants that grow to a height of 16 to 27 inches. Intermediate and border bearded irises are the same height but have different bloom seasons. The peak bloom for intermediate bearded irises must be earlier than the normal tall bearded iris bloom season (see chapter 9 on median irises).

Inbreeding. The intercrossing of genetically close individuals, often repeated self-pollinations or sibling crosses.

Irisarian. An iris-lover.

JA. Japanese iris (see chapter 18).

LA. Louisiana iris (see chapter 16).

LISA. Louisiana Iris Society of America.

Luminata. An iris flower-color pattern noted for the absence of anthocyanin pigment in the hafts and hearts of the flowers.

MDB. Miniature dwarf bearded iris (see chapter 10).

Meristem. Undifferentiated plant tissue from which cells of all types can arise. Meristem tissue is found in cambium tissue, root tips, stem tips and buds.

MTB. Miniature tall bearded iris (see chapter 9 on median irises).

PC. Pacific Coast iris (see Chapter 15).

Pedicel. The stalk of a single flower.

Peduncle. A supporting stalk for a flower cluster.

Perianth. The collective term for an iris flower's standards and falls.

Perianth tube. The slender tube that connects the ovary of an iris flower to its standards and falls.

pH. The value used to express acidity or alkalinity. A pH value of 7.0 represents neutral while lower numbers indicate acidity and higher numbers indicate alkalinity.

Pistil. The female reproductive organ of a flower. The ovary, style, style branch and stigma make up the pistil of an iris flower.

Plicata. A pattern of dotted or stitched colors on the outer edges of pastel or white iris flowers.

Pogon. An adjective or noun meaning "bearded."

Polyploid. An organism with more than two complete sets of chromosomes. Diploids have two complete sets of chromosomes. expressed as 2n.

Reverse amoena. A bearded iris flower with colored standards and white falls.

Rhizome. A modified, more or less horizontal underground stem.

Scape. A leafless flower stalk that rises from basal leaves.

SDB. Standard dwarf bearded iris (see chapter 9 on median irises).

Sepals. The falls of iris flowers are actually their sepals, but irisarians rarely use that term.

Sessile. An adjective referring to a plant without a stem or stalk.

Sheath. The part of the base of a leaf that wraps around the stem.

SIB. Siberian iris.

SIGNA. Species Iris Group of North America.

SJI. Society for Japanese Irises.

Spathe. The sheltering bract or modified leaf that encloses the flower bud. Iris spathes may be fleshy and green or papery and dry. Iris flowers may have both an inner and an outer spathe.

Species. A taxonomic concept referring to organisms with very similar genetic makeups. The exact meaning of the term is argued by taxonomists.

SPU. Spuria iris.

Stamen. The male organ of a flower that produces pollen. The pollen-bearing stamen is made up of a filament and an anther containing pollen grains.

Standards. The upper three true petals of an iris flower that are often broad and more or less erect. They make up the inner series of the perianth.

Stigma. The part of the pistil of a flower that receives pollen in fertilization. The stigma of an iris flower has a lip or ridge projecting from the inner surface of the style branch.

Style. The narrow, long part of the ovary bearing the stigma.

Taxon. Any one of the categories into which plants and animals are classified, including phylum, class, order, family, genus, species, variety.

Taxonomy. The science of the classification of plants and animals.

TB. Tall bearded iris (see chapter 8).

Tetraploid. Having four complete sets of chromosomes (4n).

Triploid. Having three complete sets of chromosomes (3n).

Variegata. A color pattern of iris flowers that features yellow standards and brownish red falls. Also an iris species, *I. variegata*, that has yellow standards and falls with reddish veining.

Variety. Botanically, the taxonomic grouping that includes individuals within a species that differ enough to be given a Latin varietal name. Also, a cultivated plant (cultivar) that has been given an identifying common name.

SELECTED BIBLIOGRAPHY

American Iris Society. *Bulletins of the American Iris Society* and its sections. Various locations, 1960–1995.

Castro, Jan Garden. *The Art & Life of Georgia O'Keeffe.* New York: Crown Publishers, 1985.

Church, Thomas D. *Gardens Are for People.* New York: McGraw-Hill, 1983.

Cranshaw, Whitney. *Pests of the West.* Golden, Colo.: Fulcrum Publishing, 1992.

Douglas, Geddes, ed. *The Iris.* The American Iris Society, 1947.

Dykes, William Rickatson. *The Genus Iris.* New York: Dover Publications, 1974.

Flint, Mary Louise. *Pests of the Garden and Small Farm: A Grower's Guide to Using Less Pesticides.* Berkeley: A N R Publications, University of California, 1990.

Gerard, John. *The Herbal* (1633 edition revised and enlarged by Thomas Johnson). New York: Dover Publications, 1975.

Gunther, Robert T. *The Greek Herbal of Dioscorides.* Oxford, England: Oxford University Press, 1934.

Hogrefe, Jeffrey. *O'Keeffe: Life & Legend.* New York: Bantam Books, 1992.

Lasher, Joan. "Vincent Van Gogh's Irises." *American Artist* (April 1992).

Mathew, Brian. *Iris.* Portland, Oreg.: Timber Press, 1990.

Mitchell, Sydney B. *Iris for Every Garden.* M. Barrows and Company, 1949.

Niswonger, Dave. Cape Iris Gardens (catalog). Cape Girardeau, Mo., 1995.

Nochlin, Linda. "Some Women Realists: Part One." *Arts Magazine* (February 1974).

Olkowski, William; Sheila Daar and Helga Olkowski. *Common-Sense Pest Control.* Taunton, Conn.: The Taunton Press, 1991.

Price, Molly. *The Iris Book.* New York: Dover Publications, 1973.

Rand, Edward Sprague, Jr. *Seventy Five Popular Flowers.* Boston: J. E. Tilton, 1870.

Tomkins, Calvin. "A Reporter at Large: Irises." *New Yorker* (April 1988).

Waddick, James W., ed. *Gardening with Iris Species.* St. Louis, Mo.: Species Iris Group of North America, 1995.

Walter, Thomas. *Flora Caroliniana.* London: Londini, 1788.

Warburton, Bee, ed. *The World of Irises.* Wichita, Kans.: The American Iris Society, second printing, 1985.

Williams, Philip A., ed. *Handbook for Judges and Show Officials.* American Iris Society, 1985.

INDEX

Index